BEACH HOMES

BEACH HOMES

From the Editors of **Fine Homebuilding**®

The Taunton Press

The Taunton Press, Inc., 63 South Main Street, PO Box 5506, Newtown, CT 06470-5506
e-mail: tp@taunton.com

Distributed by Publishers Group West

COVER DESIGN: Ann Marie Manca
INTERIOR DESIGN AND LAYOUT: Cathy Cassidy
COVER PHOTOGRAPHERS: (front cover) Roe A. Osborn, courtesy *Fine Homebuilding*, © The
Taunton Press., Inc.; (back cover) top right: Charles Miller, courtesy *Fine Homebuilding*,
© The Taunton Press., Inc.; middle row, left to right: Jefferson Kolle, courtesy *Fine
Homebuilding*, © The Taunton Press., Inc.; Charles Miller, courtesy *Fine Homebuilding*,
© The Taunton Press., Inc.; Roe A. Osborn, courtesy *Fine Homebuilding*, © The Taunton
Press., Inc.; bottom left: © Bill Sanders

Library of Congress Cataloging-in-Publication Data:

Beach homes.
     p. cm.
  ISBN 1-56158-690-0
  1. Vacation homes. 2. Waterfronts. 3. Architecture, Domestic.
TH4835.B43 2004
728.3--dc22

                              2003018558

Printed in the United States of America
10 9 8 7 6 5 4 3 2 1

Contents

Introduction

People are irresistibly drawn to the ocean. But it's hard to explain the source of this primordial tug. Does the pounding surf recall the pounding of our mothers' hearts in the womb? Or is the ocean just nice to look at, cool to listen to and fun to play in? Whatever the reason, we all dream of a house at the beach.

Designing and building a house on the coast presents special challenges. People live differently at the beach, more casually, more socially. Views are always more important than they are in a typical subdivision. And you probably won't find an outdoor shower or a sink for cleaning fish behind a house in Des Moines.

Beach houses are also different because of the harsh marine environment. The wind, the sand and the salt air will destroy a house in short order if it's not detailed properly. So if you're planning your own beach house, it makes sense to study what others have built before you. But even if you're just dreaming, what could be more inspirational than a tour through other people's beach homes?

Collected here are 17 articles from past issues of *Fine Homebuilding* magazine. Featuring some of the coolest beach houses we've ever seen, the articles are written by the people who designed the homes and offer insights into that challenging process. So enjoy a day at the beach...and don't forget the sunscreen.

—*Kevin Ireton*, editor-in-chief, *Fine Homebuilding*

Seattle Eclectic

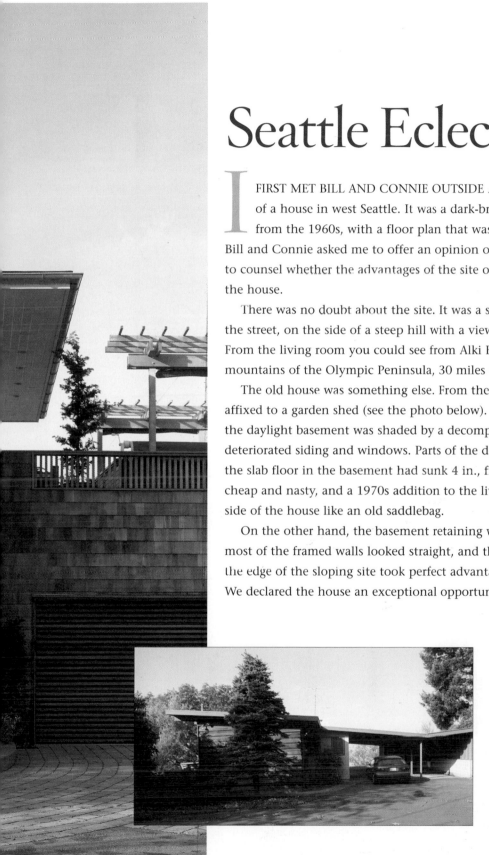

I FIRST MET BILL AND CONNIE OUTSIDE A RUN-DOWN time capsule of a house in west Seattle. It was a dark-brown and avocado disaster from the 1960s, with a floor plan that was 14 ft. wide and 60 ft. long. Bill and Connie asked me to offer an opinion of the house's condition, and to counsel whether the advantages of the site outweighed the drawbacks of the house.

There was no doubt about the site. It was a secluded spot set back from the street, on the side of a steep hill with a view to the south and west. From the living room you could see from Alki Beach on Elliot Bay to the mountains of the Olympic Peninsula, 30 miles distant.

The old house was something else. From the front, it read as a carport affixed to a garden shed (see the photo below). From the side and the rear, the daylight basement was shaded by a decomposing wood deck along with deteriorated siding and windows. Parts of the downhill-side foundation and the slab floor in the basement had sunk 4 in., finish work was uniformly cheap and nasty, and a 1970s addition to the living room drooped off the side of the house like an old saddlebag.

On the other hand, the basement retaining walls showed no cracks, most of the framed walls looked straight, and the placement of the house at the edge of the sloping site took perfect advantage of the breathtaking view. We declared the house an exceptional opportunity.

Steel canopy shelters the steps. A curvy awning of corrugated steel swoops over the concentric cast-concrete steps at the entry. The front room is an office that has an entry separate from the main house. Photo taken at A on floor plan.

Opportunity under the shed. The angular minimalism of the 1960s led to this stark structure on a superb lot in west Seattle (inset). The new house adds a second story to the existing house and replaces the carport with a garage.

The New Plan Begins with an Upstairs

With a view such as this one, the transformation agenda naturally called for a second-story addition to the house. At the west end, Bill and Connie wanted a new master bedroom over the living room to take advantage of the dramatic view. They also wanted to update the existing living spaces within an open floor plan. At the east end of the main level, a separate entrance would lead to Connie's home office (see the floor plan below). Outside, the carport would be converted into a two-car garage with a rooftop deck and a hot tub.

Instead of classifying their tastes as traditional or contemporary, Bill and Connie's primary concerns were for materials and details that would be enduring and easily maintained. They love the romanticism of Spanish-colonial architecture, and their travels in Mexico evoked visions of warm stucco walls, tiled roofs and other hand-crafted details.

My design obsessions include the ordered, rectilinear patterns found in Japanese country houses, and the finished house reflects the marriage of these two styles (see the photos on p. 4). Common to both are low-pitch tiled roofs with exposed rafters and deep eaves, which provide interesting detail and good weather protection in our often-drizzly climate. Mixing exterior-siding materials is common to Japanese country houses, and we stuck to that tradition by combining cedar shingles with accents of synthetic stucco to contrast with an olive-green concrete-tile roof.

SPECS

BEDROOMS: **2**

BATHROOMS: **3½**

HEATING SYSTEM: **Forced-air gas**

SIZE: **3,000 sq. ft.**

COST: **$130.00 per sq. ft.**
(remodel only)

COMPLETED: **1994**

LOCATION: **Seattle, Washington**

A LONG, THIN HOUSE WITH A VIEW

At the crest of a hill in west Seattle, this remodeled house began its transformation with a second-story addition to take advantage of the views of Puget Sound. The addition includes the master suite and a rooftop spa and lap pool over the garage. On the main level, an office has its own entry to maintain the privacy of the house.

Basement level   First floor   Second floor

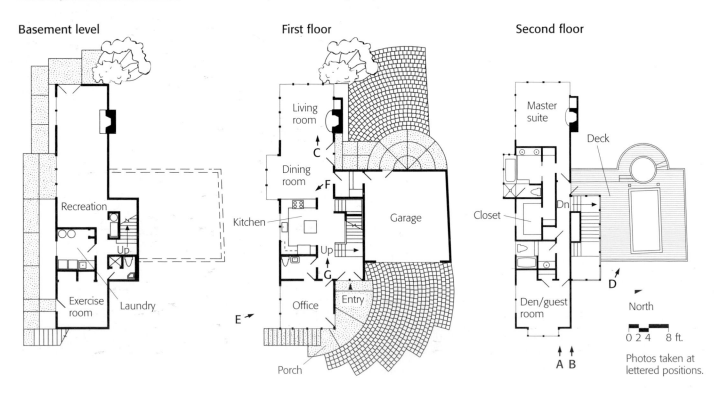

Photos taken at lettered positions.

0 2 4   8 ft.

Layering a tall wall. Repetitious patterns of windows, a bump-out for the dining room, and horizontal bands of shingles and stucco enliven the house. Photo taken at E on floor plan.

Instead of classifying their tastes as traditional or contemporary, Bill and Connie's primary concerns were for materials and details that would be enduring and easily maintained.

Structure Revealed in the Living-Room Ceiling

As work got under way on the second story, contractor Jed Johnson and his crew carefully removed the old roof decking and the timber rafters that held the decking up. These materials were then recycled into the living-room ceiling and the eaves of the new roof (see the drawing below).

The ceiling of the revamped main floor exhibits another element of Japanese design: the layering of structural components. The 4x12 fir beams support crisscrossing 2x6 floor joists, which are sheathed on top with medium-density overlay (MDO) plywood that was painted dark green (see the photo on the facing page). We omitted the traditional blocking between the ceiling joists to emphasize their long, parallel lines. The result is a delicate composition. But without some form of blocking, the ceiling assembly can also be a potentially delicate structure in an earthquake or under high winds. However, adding rows of solid blocking would diminish the effect of the ceiling. So we used diagonal steel rods instead. The rods are threaded through the beams and attached to opposing walls by way of custom-fabricated steel connectors, eliminating the need for us to have put solid blocking between the floor joists.

Energy-Saving Strategies and Structural Innovations Expand the View

The long, narrow plan is punctuated with lots of windows, opening the house to water views on three sides. The Washington State Energy Code requires houses of conventional construction to limit total window and door area to no more than 21% of the floor area of the heated living spaces. With added floor insulation, higher-performing wood

CUTAWAY TO STRUCTURE AND DETAIL

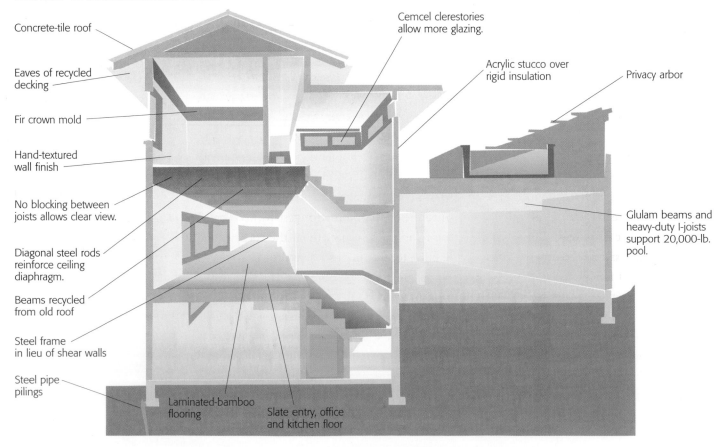

Concrete-tile roof

Eaves of recycled decking

Fir crown mold

Hand-textured wall finish

No blocking between joists allows clear view.

Diagonal steel rods reinforce ceiling diaphragm.

Beams recycled from old roof

Steel frame in lieu of shear walls

Steel pipe pilings

Laminated-bamboo flooring

Slate entry, office and kitchen floor

Cemcel clerestories allow more glazing.

Acrylic stucco over rigid insulation

Privacy arbor

Glulam beams and heavy-duty I-joists support 20,000-lb. pool.

A view worth the trouble. A wall-to-wall expanse of windows overlooks Puget Sound and the distant mountains. The dark columns between the windows are the vertical members of a steel frame that allowed the extensive glazing. Above the windows, insulated-fiberglass panels admit diffused daylight. Photo taken at C on floor plan.

doors and a high-efficiency furnace, we were able to reach 30% glazing to maximize the views and natural light.

Part of our efficiency was found in the use of Cemcel, a laminated-fiberglass panel (see sources on p. 10). Cemcel panels resemble the rice-paper-and-wood divided lites found in shoji screens (see the photo above). But unlike rice paper, Cemcel has the strength and safety of tempered glass and U-values that range from 0.40 to as low as 0.25, depending on thickness and filling. Cemcel isn't cheap: Costs start at around $25 per sq. ft. for the material, which means $250 or more to glaze a single door. I've used it a lot in skylights because the translucency is good at hiding dirt and scratches. In Bill and Connie's house, using

Cemcel allowed us to gain daylight in places where we couldn't use windows without violating the energy code.

Maximizing the number of windows presented another problem. We now had a tall, thin house on a hill in a seismic-four zone (serious earthquake potential) looking south into the teeth of our strongest winds. The new windows—especially at the corners—eliminated essential shear walls needed to brace the house against wind and earthquake loads.

Instead of relying on conventional plywood shear walls at the corners, we braced the house with a steel frame. Built from 8-in. wide flange steel I-beams, the frame was welded together in place. The frame becomes a visible element in the house as it

The long, narrow plan is punctuated with lots of windows, opening the house to water views on three sides.

SOURCES

Cemcel Corp.
San Pablo, CA 94806
510-235-9911

A. B. Chance
573-682-5521
www.abchance.com

Michelangelo Inc./Michelangelo Marble
206-767-6549
www.michelangelomarble.com

extends from the top of the concrete foundation wall to the top floor plate. The columns of the frame are visible inside the living room and master bedroom. A similar frame reinforces the front wall.

A sweeping steel canopy shelters the front door (see the photo on p. 4). The canopy frame is suspended by steel rods, and it is covered with corrugated decking. To make a clear break from traditional housing precedents, we chose the steel both to promote the durability of the structure and to reinforce the contemporary virtues of the design.

Holding up the Slab

The dips in the downhill foundation and the slab proved to be less of a concern than everyone imagined. To prevent further settling of the house when the new floor was added, we installed pneumatically driven steel-pipe pilings on 2-ft. centers along the 60-ft. wall (see the left drawing on p. 6).

Each piling was then affixed to the foundation with Chance Anchors (see sources). These anchors are steel brackets that grab the foundation with epoxied bolts. Adding the anchors stabilized the wall, allowing us to build atop it without fear of further settling.

Let's Put a Pool on the Roof

Our first owner-initiated change order was the lap pool over the garage (see the photo below). This isn't as audacious as it sounds. The swimming spa is much smaller than a conventional lap pool (jets create an adjustable current of water to swim against) and therefore can be economically maintained at a temperature that allows year-round use in our mild climate. Such a spa does, however, weigh about 20,000 lb. when full of water.

After some delays for engineering and permit adjustments, we poured new footings, beefed up the outboard garage wall and installed some large glulam beams. Commercial-grade plywood joists topped with conventional-plywood decking span the big beams. And a torch-down single-ply membrane protects the roof.

A Variety of Textures and Colors Inside

In contrast to the hard, smooth steel canopy that arcs over the entry, the interior walls are finished with hand-troweled plaster, layered in the heavy textures common to Spanish-colonial houses. We chose slate flooring for the entry, Connie's office and the kitchen (see the left photo on the facing page). At about $12 per sq. ft. installed, slate is relatively affordable. It's a low-maintenance finish, and the earthy colors of the slate look good alongside bamboo flooring in the living room and dining room. The bamboo, which is made up of laminated strips,

Laps atop the garage. A small heated pool with swim jets turns the roof of the garage into an exercise spa. Photo taken at D on floor plan.

The dining table is almost in the trees. A stovetop counter overlooks the dining area. The doors in the upper cabinets have seeded glass panels, which reflect light in fractured lines. Photo taken at F on floor plan.

Starting at the kitchen, the ceiling sets the style. Rows of ceiling joists urge the eye toward the view and emphasize the linear soul of the house. The diagonal steel rods help to reinforce the ceiling. Beefy rafters from the original roof reappear here as the ceiling beams. Photo taken at G on floor plan.

resembles maple in color. It is hard, is dimensionally stable and can be finished with water-base or solvent-base finishes (see sources).

Fir trim wraps around the windows inside, repeating the honey color of the ceiling framing on the main level. In the living room, a polished-granite hearth anchors a cast-concrete fireplace surround framed by a mosaic of inlaid stone.

A counter separates the dining area (see the right photo above) from the kitchen; the counter includes the cooktop and upper cabinets. Panels of seeded glass in the upper-cabinet doors create ripply lines of light and dark that resemble bubbles, or more appropriately, raindrops.

Lane Williams is an architect in Seattle, WA.

Dueling Towers
on the Carolina Coast

I F TWO COOKS IN THE SAME KITCHEN IS A RECIPE FOR TROUBLE,
then two architects designing separate halves of the same building
should spell disaster. But just the opposite happened when I collabo-
rated with Dan Costa, a Boston-based architect and friend, on a project
to create a public beach access for a new resort village planned for Bald
Head Island, North Carolina. Located 35 miles south of Wilmington,
Bald Head Island and its rugged shoals form the notorious Cape Fear.

A landmark for land and sea. Built to mark the public access to the beach beyond, the towers are a keystone structure for the seaside village. Boat captains have come to use the towers as a range to help navigate the waters. Photo taken at A on floor plan.

Two Tall Towers Flank the Path to the Beach

Dan and I came up with the idea for the towers during a planning session with Kent Mitchell, the island's developer, late in 1993. Kent, who is also an architect, wanted to create a distinctive building that would point the way to the beach access for his new island community, Harbour Village. But local development rules limited the amount of land for the beach access, and the cost of building a large community structure would have been prohibitive. So Dan and I volunteered to design and build two single-family

SOUTH TOWER (TIJUCA)

NORTH TOWER (RAPUNZEL)

FOR EACH TOWER

BEDROOMS: **2**

BATHROOMS: **2**

HEATING SYSTEM: **Heat pump/air conditioning**

SIZE: **1,200 sq. ft.**

COST (north tower): **$100.00 per sq. ft.**

COST (south tower): N/A

COMPLETED: **1994**

LOCATION: **Bald Head, North Carolina**

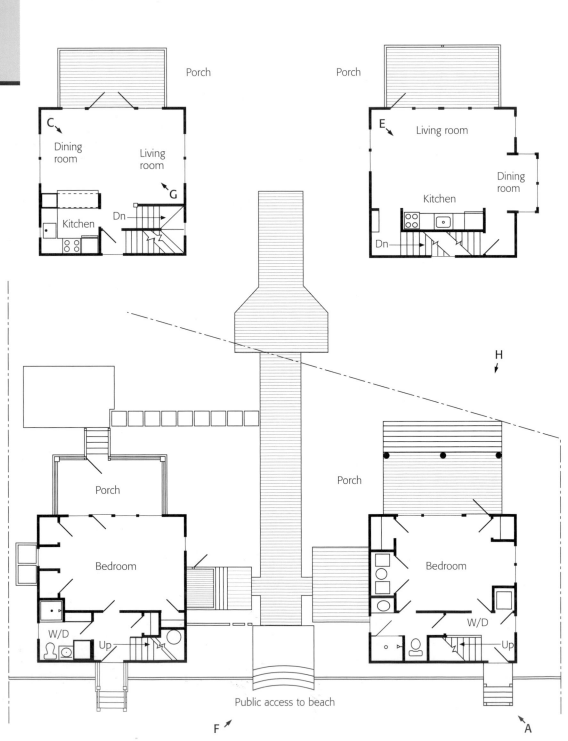

TWO DIFFERENT TOWERS GROW UP AROUND TWO DIFFERENT STAIRCASES

Each architect began with a different idea on how best to climb the towers' three floors. The southern tower has a staircase that winds around one corner, creating an L-shaped floor space. The stairs in the northern tower are stacked in straight runs, leaving a large rectangular space on each floor.

North

0 2 4   8 ft.

Photos taken at lettered positions.

houses that would create a kind of gateway to the beach in exchange for a break on the lots. The towers (see the photo on pp. 12–13) would be connected with a trellis and a walkway to carry the public over the fragile dunes to the beach.

Different Stairs Create Different Designs

For Dan and me, designing the towers became an instant source of friendly competition. The only rules of the game were that each tower had to be three stories high with a hip roof and that each would be built on a 20-ft. by 20-ft. footprint. We did not look at each other's plans until they were nearly completed so that we wouldn't influence each other's design. Each of the towers was designed with a bedroom and a bathroom on the first floor; kitchen, living space and dining space on the second floor; and the master bedroom and bath on the top floor. We also chose similar materials for the exterior roof and siding of each tower. But beyond these few basic items, not much else is the same between the two buildings.

The differences between the towers begin with two contrasting stair decisions (see the floor plans on the facing page). Dan's tower (the southern tower with the dark-green accents) has a stairway that winds its way around one corner, creating an L-shaped floor space. My tower (the northern tower with light-green and yellow accents) has two stacked, straight runs of stairs that leave a rectangular-shaped space on each level.

Dan's corner stair allows for a central entry on the first floor and a discreet kitchen separate from the large living and dining area on the second floor (see the bottom photo at right). With my stacked stair, the entry is off center, and the kitchen is linear, running almost the entire length of one second-floor wall (see the top photo at right). The two

Straight stairs behind the kitchen leave an open space for kitchen, living room and a well-lit dining area. Photo taken at E on floor plan.

A corner stairway sets off a comfortable kitchen space. Photo taken at C on floor plan.

different interior layouts are reflected in the different exterior window patterns.

The towers' different personalities are even more apparent from the interior treatments. Dan's tower is named Tijuca, after a beach in Brazil where Dan and his sister Margot (who is also a part owner) summered as children. The simple woodwork, exposed ceiling joists, painted-beadboard paneling and furnishings seem to recall a far-off, simpler time.

I called my tower Rapunzel after the long-haired girl in the children's fairy tale who was held prisoner in a secluded tower. Rapunzel's interior is bright and brash with walls painted in bold, primary colors and simple moldings.

I Say Po-tay-to, You Say Po-tah-to

Although the window patterns are probably the most obvious exterior difference between the two towers, there are many other details that Dan and I included that complement each other's designs while creating a comfortable asymmetry.

Although we had agreed to use hip roofs on our towers, we never discussed overhangs. Dan designed Tijuca's roof with wide overhangs supported by large painted brackets that hint at the exposed structure inside. The larger overhangs on Dan's tower also create a slightly shallower pitch on the hip roof, but the eaves of the two towers are lined up at the same height. The porches on the two towers also received different treatments. I chose not to put a roof over my second-floor porch to take advantage of the afternoon sun. However, I built solid sidewalls to cut down on the island's persistent breezes. The roof over Dan's porch steps down nicely from the wide overhangs that are above, and his more traditional railings create an intimate space for cool rocking-chair evenings (see the photo below).

The porches on the first floor are even more different. My porch is approached with stairs that run its full width, drawing

Covered porch expands the living room. French doors open a window from the living room to the sea. The roof and traditional railing turn the porch into an intimate space that beckons you to sit and rock. Photo taken at G on floor plan.

Trellis and walkway bridge towering personalities. Beachgoers who use this walkway experience the character of each building. The railings offer a straight, steady transition to sea on one side while the other side mirrors the playful lines of the dunes. Photo taken at F on floor plan.

the eye into a visual ascent of the tower. While I supported the porch structure with full cedar logs for a bold, rustic flavor, Dan's screened-in porch with its discreet entry and simple lines makes for a more private, quiet outdoor room.

The contrasting, complementary elements of our two designs are perhaps most evident in the trellis and public walkway where the two impish twins are joined (see the photo above). As you stroll along the boardwalk, the fence and railing on Tijuca's side have strong classic details. The solid

top rail creates a powerful horizontal line that points toward the horizon of the sea beyond. Rapunzel's fence, on the other hand, undulates randomly in a playful mimic of the surrounding dunes.

A 360° View, the Essence of the Tower Experience

At 1,200 sq. ft. per tower, these houses aren't exactly huge, but from the outside, the twin aspect of the towers doubles their impact. However, inside Dan and I had to work to make the houses feel as large as

Exposed framing, painted beadboard. The interior of this tower recalls New England beach houses with exposed rafters and wood walls. A bathroom with an inside window is on the top floor. Photo taken at B on floor plan.

Plaster walls and playful colors. A starry sky makes for a fanciful canopy above the master bedroom. Photo taken at D on floor plan.

possible. And nowhere is this effort more apparent than in the third-floor bedrooms.

We each wrapped the third floors with a band of windows to take full advantage of the elevation and the view. Being able to look out to the horizon in every direction is at the heart of the tower experience. Also, the windows offer uniform lighting and refreshing cross ventilation throughout the course of the day.

Both Dan and I elected to have cathedral ceilings in the third-floor bedrooms, Dan staying with a theme of exposed rafters and beadboard (see the left photo above). I chose to plaster the ceiling and paint it evening blue with gold stars scattered all over (see the right photo above). Dan partitioned off the small section of the L formed by stairs for a third-floor bathroom. He put a window in the partition over the bed to let light from the bathroom filter into the bedroom.

My stair system left me with a large open space on the third floor, but there was no easy way to create a separate bathroom and still have the sweeping tower views I desired. So I opted for what I call the Poconos approach. I placed a whirlpool bath in the middle of the room between two towerlike structures, one of which forms a private area for the commode.

High Winds and Close Calls

Many people question the prudence of building any sort of structure in a hurricane-prone area, much less a pair of tall, skinny buildings such as these. As architect as well as homeowner, I must confess that romance was the guiding force behind both the location and the design of the towers.

To counterbalance any romantic notions that might have been dancing in our heads, Dan and I made sure that we followed all recommendations made by our structural engineer, Rob O'Briant. The towers were

Full-width stairs for a grand rear entry. Stairs as wide as the rustic, open porch invite the eye to climb up the northern tower. The bump-out on the second floor is an asymmetrical echo of the porch roof on the other tower. Built to withstand 110-mph winds, the two sentinel towers were twice subjected to 100-plus mph winds and have so far escaped serious damage. Photo taken at H on floor plan.

built to withstand 110-mph winds, and hurricanes Bertha and Fran, as well as two lesser tropical storms, put Rob's structural expertise to the test.

The eyes of both hurricanes passed right over the towers, and a bolt of lightning from Bertha struck my weather station,

freezing it forever at a wind speed of 99 mph, its highest possible reading. With some inexplicable luck and with much gratitude to Rob, our towers emerged from the storms with no major damage.

Chuck Dietsche is an architect who splits his time between Wilmington, NC, and Bald Head Island.

Building by the Water

S
NAILS, SEA URCHINS, ROCK CRABS, HERMIT CRABS, BLADDER wrack, kelp, spartina grass, mussels, oysters, barnacles, limpets, starfish—all are marine organisms that have various means to cling tenaciously to rocks or withstand constant exposure to sun, wind and water. Humans who choose to live by the ocean have to make do with potentially fragile houses. As a Boston architect, I've built numerous houses on creeks, lakes and the ocean, and I've learned a lot about the details that are required for a project on the water.

A few years ago, I was asked to design a house along the rocky coast of Massachusetts in Gloucester, a small town still known as a fishing port. My clients, Maggie and Joe Rosa, work in the biotech industry, obviously a very different profession than fishing, but they understood the unspoiled beauty of Gloucester. Therefore, their first and most important program requirement was that the house fit in. For a house to fit in, I believe that the aesthetics of building and functions of living must work together; the Rosa house is a good example of how this process can work along the water.

A dramatic view and a perilous site. Located at the edge of the Atlantic, the house was designed to offer wonderful views and to protect its inhabitants from the elements (inset). Photo taken at B on floor plan. **Ocean views, while hardly spare**, are deliberately revealed where they'll be most appreciated, the living room, the kitchen, and the master bedroom. Photo taken at A on floor plan..

SPECS

BEDROOMS: 4

BATHROOMS: 2½

HEATING SYSTEM: Gas-fired

hot water

SIZE: 3,433 sq. ft. (includes garage)

COST: $115.00 per sq. ft.

COMPLETED: 1994

LOCATION: Gloucester,

Massachusetts

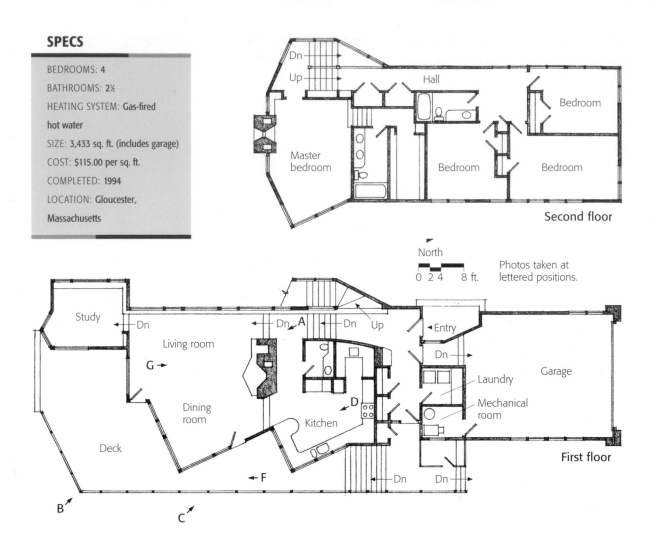

Second floor

North

0 2 4   8 ft.

Photos taken at
lettered positions.

First floor

We tried to design the house so that the floor plan developed dramatic tension.

What Determines a Floor Plan?

After my first visit to the Rosa site, I began to think of any potential hurdles we would have to jump over on our way to designing the house. Most water sites come with regulations, ranging from the local conservation commission to the Army Corps of Engineers. These regulations can have a major impact on the design of a house, depending on the house's proximity to water. Most often, such regulations affect the siting of the house, sometimes determining the view. And the view is the reason that my clients almost always build along the water.

In general, though, it is the site and its dramatic potential that generate my initial ideas about the plan (see the floor plan above). I believe that any properly sited house should take advantage of its surroundings and that any good floor plan should not reveal the whole drama of the surroundings all at once. The floor plan should be choreographed so that spaces such as the entry are only introductions of what is to come, while at least one space should be what we in the office call the "oh, my God" (OMG for short), giving you the full drama of the site and revealing the reason you're building there in the first place. All the rooms in the house don't need to have a great view or even face the water. It may seem contradictory, but I think this is a way to take full advantage of a site. The result is a more interesting plan.

The Rosa house is parallel to the water's edge, not because we planned it that way but because the conservation commission required it for setbacks. That initial requirement, together with some spectacular views, shaped the Rosa house plan (see the floor plan on the facing page). The living room, the kitchen (see the top photo at right), and the master bedroom have the great views, the other rooms less so, and the entry has no view of the water at all. The parallel position of the house could have allowed us to provide every room with a dramatic view, but we didn't think that was appropriate. Instead, we tried to design the house so that the floor plan developed dramatic tension. The entry of the Rosa house is recessed and hidden from the street. This aspect gives the arrival to the house an almost mysterious quality. Even after entering the house, you are still not aware of the potential view. Only after finding your way down several small flights of stairs (see the bottom photo at right) do you discover the real reason the house is there in the first place: the view of the ocean (see the photo on p. 21). Giving it all away at once would be like having the main course before the appetizers, and it is one of the reasons I think many large suburban homes are so unappealing. They want you to know what they're about all at once, without an introduction first, some discussion, then a proposal. Good floor plans on any good site are the same way.

Foundations Along the Shore Are Never Easy

Building along the water often means dealing with special subsurface-soil conditions. It may mean sand or soup for soil, or as with the Rosa house, it may mean nothing but rock. Each condition requires a special response and may even be an advantage.

Kitchen's granite countertop echoes the geology just outside the window. The author designed the floor plan to jut out in the kitchen and in the living room to accentuate the view of the surging water. Photo taken at D on floor plan.

Floor plan follows the level of the granite below. Rather than treat the ledge as a hindrance, the author used the slope of the ledge to establish the flow of the rooms in a series of gradual steps. The same ledge found its way into the fireplace design. Photo taken at G on floor plan.

Taking advantage of the site. Instead of dynamiting the granite ledge, the author chose to keep as much of the rock intact as possible and allow the slope to determine the levels of the first-floor rooms. As a result, the interior floor plan drops in gradual steps from the entrance to the dining and living rooms, creating a subtly dramatic entrance to the grand view of the ocean. Photo taken at C on floor plan.

I remember clearly on that first site visit watching Maggie and Joe Rosa drawn almost magnetically to the flat portions of ledge at the edge of the water. I saw then how important it was to make the house feel as if it actually sat on the ledge and how we might use some of that ledge on the interior of the house (see the photo on the facing page). With contractor David Pywell, we tried to retain most of the ledge without blasting, with the exception of a small crown of ledge under the garage-slab location.

Of course, nothing is as easy as it seems. We first had to find an accurate survey so that we could design our plan around the existing ledge. We made a number of site visits to position the foundation and to adjust the various floor heights. Next, we had to pin portions of the foundation to the ledge because it is generally cheaper to pin the foundation wall to the ledge than it is to remove the ledge for footings.

Surface water doesn't drain through ledge. The siting of the foundation actually worked against the natural drainage of the site because the long side of the Rosa foundation was parallel to the ocean and generally up slope. To solve this problem, we provided an opening in the foundation wall under the house to allow for site drainage down the slope and a prefabricated drainage pipe along the entire length of the long wall foundation draining to both ends. In addition, because the house was built either on a slab over ledge or over a crawlspace, we didn't have to worry about basement-wall leakage.

Anticipating High Winds and Wind-Driven Rain

For those who live by the water, there seems to be a contradictory tendency to want to expose as much of the house to the elements as possible but at the same time to shelter yourself from the elements. Even modern

windows and other technologies don't give us a clear answer to that contradiction, but over the years I've tended to come down on the side of sheltering. Wind-driven rain does funny things. Water can actually be blown vertically or even sucked into an opening, however small, because of differential pressures. I've learned to appreciate water that blows up into wide soffits and then drains from the same soffit rather than to the interior of the house. In New England, the same large soffits can help to prevent ice dams in the same way by allowing melting ice to drain out from the soffit rather than into the wall.

Of course, these large overhangs require a certain amount of strength because of the hurricane-force winds common along the ocean. Wood framing has its limits, particularly if you want to keep the depth of the framing member small, so I don't mind using a little steel now and then. My rule is to try to keep the steel members' size manageable for the crew doing the work. The Rosa house has steel ridge beams and a few steel members running perpendicular to the ridge beams, which help to prevent wind uplift of the large unsupported roof overhangs facing the water.

But hurricanes don't just blow off roofs, they can blow over houses, too. The Rosa house has steel cross bracing underneath to brace the house and to allow for the

... any properly sited house should take advantage of its surroundings and any good floor plan should not reveal the whole drama of the surroundings all at once.

cantilevered decks. The bracing sits on haunches and is bolted into the foundation wall below. I've never liked to expose structure on the exterior of a house, so we concealed the exposed bracing with the skirt of the deck. Other hidden structural techniques include the mandatory use of hurricane anchors between the rafters and the top wall plate; these hurricane anchors form a second line of defense against uplift.

Exterior Details are Elegant and Weatherproof

Good design and good construction techniques are inseparable, especially along the water. On the Rosa house the cedar wall shingles are spaced so that a single course with 5-in. exposure alternates with three courses of 3-in. exposure each. This tightening of the wall shingles provides better wind and water protection and reinforces an overall horizontal view of the house. As with most common-sense detailing, the result is also elegant (see the photo below).

Another spacing pattern that may not be so obvious is the 4-in. roof-shingle exposure. As with the wall, this provides for better wind and water protection and gives the roof a more refined look.

These design details come with some hidden construction techniques. The roof shingles are "hurricane-nailed," meaning they're nailed with five nails instead of four and nailed closer to the tab edge; the tabs are then glued down with roofing cement. We installed a self-adhesive bituminous membrane on all of the vulnerable portions of the roof, especially over the large overhangs and in the valleys. We also used lead-coated copper flashing throughout to protect against the cedar contact. As a final precaution, any exterior seams or joints that might allow any water seepage were care-fully sealed with a judicious amount of caulking.

Choosing Finishes and Hardware That Will Survive Salt, Wind and Water

If I'm dealing with a wood house, woods with natural preservatives such as cypress, cedar and redwood are my first choice. I also don't believe in using paint on houses along the water, except in special circumstances such as a main-entry door. A natural finish or a stained finish is best. Staining a house gives it a more uniform appearance over time, as opposed to letting the wood weather naturally. Stainless-steel nails are always our siding fastener of choice.

It goes without saying that the choice of windows for a house along the water is extremely important. Use the best windows you can find that have good factory-service support. For the Rosa house, I chose Marvin wood windows and doors that had an aluminum cladding with a factory-finish paint made to stand up against severe weather (see sources on the facing page). The hope is that

Small windows give a measure of privacy and make an unassuming facade. The side of the house that faces the street offers visitors no hint of the drama that gradually unfolds on the other side of the front door. Photo taken at E on floor plan.

they will never have to be painted again. The only other option might have been a vinyl-clad window, but in this case we preferred the sizing and quality of the aluminum-clad windows. I also prefer windows that come with integral flashing/flanges when I'm building along the water. Again, we caulked behind the flanges.

Door and window hardware take a special beating. Corrosion, especially salt corrosion, can destroy the working mechanisms of otherwise good hardware. Many window and door manufacturers now sell stainless-steel options for their hardware, but it is an expensive option. An alternative is to apply energy or storm panels or to keep the number of operable devices on windows to a minimum. In other words, use fixed windows when you can and operable windows only when you must.

Stainless steel makes a strong and elegant deck railing that resists salt corrosion. The railing is lightweight and easy to maintain, and it doesn't interrupt the view of the ocean from the living hall. Photo taken at F on floor plan.

Decks and Outdoor Spaces

Decks and other outdoor spaces are important. No one builds near the water to stay indoors all the time. Even on a foggy day, it can be fun to sit outside and enjoy the sound of the crashing waves or the foghorn in the distance. I believe a good deck adds to the feel of a good living space by extending it to the outside.

Exterior handrails can also be another difficult finish area. Contemporary codes generally require a lot of verticals or horizontals to comply. If you build your rails of wood, it means a lot of material, joints, connections and staining. At the Rosa house we had the vertical support balusters built by Joe Rosa's brother from stainless steel and used simple ¼-in. stainless-steel boat cables and hardware for the horizontals (see the photo above). This choice of rail materials also coincided with a wonderful aesthetic solution because it provided an almost completely open view of the water from the living hall.

A detail not talked about as much is the relation of the deck to grade. It's just as important that that transition be smooth. In the Rosa house, the transition from the living-room floor to the deck is only a few inches at the threshold, and the transition from the deck to a portion of the rock is only two steps. The transition from living space to deck to grade is never abrupt.

Building and living by the water is a privilege not all of us can enjoy. If you have the opportunity, make the most of it. If you treat a building by the water as just another house that could be built anywhere, you're likely to pay the consequences in time.

Jeremiah Eck is the author of *The Distinctive Home: A Vision of Timeless Design* (The Taunton Press, Inc., 2003), a fellow of the American Institute of Architects, a former lecturer in architecture at the Harvard Design School, and a landscape painter. Paul McNeely was the project architect.

SOURCES

Marvin Windows & Doors
800-346-5128
www.marvin.com

A Little House with Rich Spaces

A NEARBY HIGH SCHOOL HAS AN INGENIOUS APPROACH to teaching basic construction methods. Each year a private sponsor is found to purchase the materials for a building project. For an extra 10% of the cost, the sponsor then receives a fully framed, prefabricated building that is ready to be erected on the site of their choice. In the past, projects have included cabins, carports, worksheds and other wood-framed structures of similar bulk and complexity.

A couple of years ago the class was set to build a garage when the sponsor suddenly withdrew. The class of 18 students was left without a project on which to develop practical framing skills. By the time my architectural office got a call to see if we had any ideas, the class had already started, and the students were growing restless.

Into the breach jumped one of my firm's clients. He owns a small farm on Pender, one of the Gulf Islands off the coast of Vancouver, B. C., Canada, and he'd been thinking about building a guest cottage. The cottage would provide accommodations for staff and colleagues from his publishing business, as well as for occasional guests and seasonal farm help.

My office has done a number of low-budget houses, including a couple of forays into the realm of affordable-housing competitions. Based on those experiences, my colleagues and I decided to apply our knowledge of modular-construction techniques to this particular project. The house we came up with is based on the universal module: the 4x8 sheet of plywood. As a result, the house is basically a plywood box. But even though it encompasses a scant 900 sq. ft., this little two-and-a-half story house is a barrack with aspirations.

A simple cube with cutouts. A glazed canopy over the entry lets the sunlight reach inside the house where it can warm the concrete floors in the kitchen. The skylight at the peak of the roof illuminates the loft. The asbestos-cement roof provides a fireproof skin. Photo taken at A on floor plan.

Two-and-a-half Levels

In plan, the modular layout of the cottage can be seen as a series of squares and rectangles. The rigid, gridlike arrangement of the modules simplified the layout of the foundation and made for efficient use of building materials.

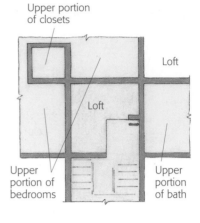

Upper portion of closets

Loft

Loft

Upper portion of bedrooms

Upper portion of bath

SPECS

BEDROOMS: **2 plus a loft**

BATHROOMS: **1**

HEATING SYSTEM: **Wood, electric backup**

SIZE: **900 sq. ft.**

COST: **$45.00 per sq. ft. (donated labor)**

COMPLETED: **1986**

LOCATION: **Pender Island, B.C. Canada**

North

0 2 4   8 ft.

Photos taken at lettered positions.

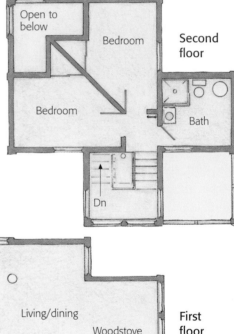

Open to below

Bedroom

Second floor

Bedroom

Bath

Dn

Living/dining

Woodstove

First floor

Up

Kitchen

Entry

Canopy overhead

Section A

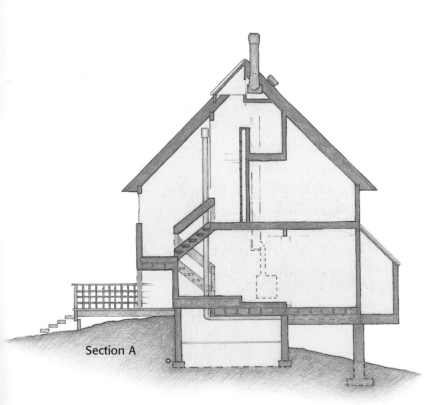

Section A

The Plan

The main floor contains a living and dining space on one level and a kitchen with a sheltered entry on another (see the floor plan on the facing page). In the living area, a pair of built-in couches tucks into the corner. Lit by windows and skylights, the corner is a cantilevered bay that projects beyond the line of the columns that bear the weight of the perimeter walls. The sloped glazing over the couches and the vaulted ceiling in the living room lend an expansive quality to what are actually small spaces (see the photo at right). Upstairs, two compact bedrooms overlook the living room and share the large bathroom. A kid-sized loft, lit by skylights and reached by a ladder, adds another bunk and more open space to the stair volume.

Because the house is on a beautiful site, you want to be outdoors as much as possible. With that in mind, a large south-facing deck connects the house at the dining room to the hillside.

Modules in the Parking Lot

As requested by the instructor, Bjorn Hilstad, we designed the house to be built with platform-framing techniques. The house is made of 2x4 frames covered with T-111 plywood. After several sessions studying the working drawings and tallying up the necessary materials, Hilstad's class started cutting up the materials in the comfort of an enclosed shop. Most of the panels are 8 ft. tall and 8 ft. wide. When covered with plywood on just one side, panels this size are still pretty maneuverable. Hilstad's class affixed the exterior plywood to the stick-framed walls. The interior walls, which are also T-111 plywood, were installed after the plumbing and wiring runs were completed.

The class worked through the fall fabricating the panels. Then they got a dose of construction reality by assembling the

Built-ins by the bay. The combination of sloped glazing and a vaulted ceiling impart a lofty feeling to what is actually a small space. Photo taken at B on floor plan.

pieces in the school parking lot during a drizzly Vancouver winter (see the photo on p. 32). A wood base served as a temporary foundation for the house, and the panels were tacked together with duplex nails so that they could be disassembled easily.

The horizontal and vertical seams between panels align. In the finished cottage the vertical edges are covered with 1x2 battens, and the horizontals are separated with Z-flashings. Rough-sawn 2x8s conceal the seams where the walls come together at outside corners.

To spread the spirit of learning-by-doing a little wider, we arranged for an 18-wheel truck—piloted by a student driver—to transport the parts of the house to the site. The entire shell—numbered and disassembled— was packed into the truck's cargo bay. Then the truck headed for the ferry boat to the Gulf Islands.

The Gulf Island ferry's combination entry/exit ramp requires all vehicles to

Lit by windows and skylights, the corner is a cantilevered bay that projects beyond the line of the columns that bear the weight of the perimeter walls.

Parked in the lot. The prefab panels were test fitted in the high-school parking lot atop temporary platforms. The panels were attached to one another with duplex nails for easy disassembly. The 8-ft. by 8-ft. panels were then trucked to the site and assembled by the class.

board at the bow and then circle around the vessel to exit. However, big trucks can't do this: They have to back onto the ferry. The pressure of backing a fully loaded driver-training semi-trailer into the darkness of a yawning ferry hull was not lost on the cheering passengers. The task eventually fell to the driving instructor.

Energy Saving on a Tiny Footprint

While the students were busy loading the 8x8 panels into the truck, a crew from the island began clearing the site. They had to take out a cedar tree and a large fir that stood within the perimeter of the house. Both trees were hauled off to the farm's simple

The concrete floors and the plywood walls are industrial strength and in keeping with the working nature of the site.

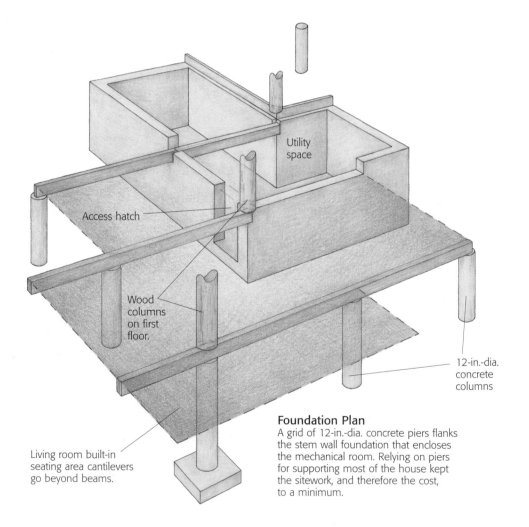

Utility space

Access hatch

Wood columns on first floor.

12-in.-dia. concrete columns

Living room built-in seating area cantilevers go beyond beams.

Foundation Plan
A grid of 12-in.-dia. concrete piers flanks the stem wall foundation that encloses the mechanical room. Relying on piers for supporting most of the house kept the sitework, and therefore the cost, to a minimum.

but well-used sawmill to be turned into building materials for the cottage.

We try to keep excavations to a minimum on sloping, hard-to-reach sites. Instead of bulldozing a flat pad for a house, we would rather leave the terrain in its natural contours and build a house on piers (see the drawing on the facing page). The uphill corner of this cottage sits atop a stem-wall foundation that encloses a head-high mechanical room for the central vacuum and the water heater. The rest of the house is carried by 12-in.-dia. cast-concrete piers.

The house is heated by a woodstove that's centrally located against the half-wall that separates the kitchen from the living area (see the photo at right). The woodstove puts out enough heat for all but the coldest days, when the backup electric-baseboard heating kicks in. But that's only a last resort. A fair amount of solar heat is collected by the concrete floor in the kitchen, as the sun streams through the glazed canopy that shelters the entry.

To take advantage of the heat that collects at the top of the stairs, we included a heat-redistribution system. It is simply an 8-in. dia. air duct that extends to within a foot of the skylight in the loft. A two-speed fan mounted in the top of the duct sends the warm air back to the first floor, where it's directed to a register under the stairs and to another register between the sliding doors and the dining table.

Getting rid of the heat in the summer is more of a problem than keeping it in during the winter. Right now the heat is exhausted directly through a hand-operated roof vent. But experience has shown that this 12-in. by 8-in. vent is too small to do the job without a mechanical assist.

The Budget

We had $40,000 to spend on this house, and we did. That works out to about $45 per sq.

Concrete floors. The exposed-aggregate concrete floor in the kitchen spreads around the corner to the pad for the woodstove. A galvanized duct to the right redistributes heated air from the loft to a couple of downstairs heating registers. Photo taken at C on floor plan.

ft., which would have been closer to $65 or $70 per sq. ft. without the donated labor of the high-school class. The materials we used were relatively inexpensive and should hold up well. The concrete floors and the plywood walls are industrial strength and in keeping with the working nature of the site.

So too is the asbestos-cement roof. But in retrospect, I don't think we would specify such a roof again. Our client wanted a fireproof roof skin, and from a durability point of view, the choice of asbestos-cement roofing made sense. The product is essentially inert and affords long-term, maintenance-free protection from the elements. However, the possibility of asbestos inhalation required the installers to wear proper respiratory gear, clean their work clothes meticulously and continually hose down the work area to minimize dust. If we had to do it again, we'd specify fire-retardant treated wood shingles.

The comparative comfort and the newness of the cottage have overshadowed the farmhouse a bit. Now the old place seems a little too rustic, but the owner doesn't seem to mind. The earliest arrival on weekend outings gets first dibs on lodgings, and that's usually the owner.

Barry Griblin is an architect in West Vancouver, B. C., Canada.

The House on Windy Beach

IN 1989, I MET A BUILDER AT A LUMBERYARD OVERLOOKING the Northern California coastline. We started talking about his projects, and he told me about one potential job that had him tied in knots. "I've been asked to bid on an Obie Bowman project," he said. "I don't know whether I should. If I get it, it could be the most important project of my career. On the other hand, it could put me out of business."

Such is the reputation of Obie Bowman, architect of some of coastal California's most memorable houses. Even though the houses are typically modest in size, they sizzle with originality. Pushing the edges of conventional construction techniques, they often include unconventional materials. A Bowman house might have boulders in the bathroom or a layer of sod on the roof. One house has a brick fireplace that starts out in a running-bond pattern, then morphs into an abstract gumbo of clinker bricks. As you can imagine, these projects can be as tough to bid as they are to build.

Glowing like a lantern, the view loft cantilevers over the deck. Photos taken at A and B on floor plan.

Site-specific design is another Bowman hall-mark. His buildings reflect the nature of the landscape they occupy, resulting in a portfolio of houses completely different from one another. This one, overlooking a majestic stretch of desolate Oregon coastline, is no exception (see the photo on p. 35).

Shaped by Elemental Forces

When the Oregon coast is pounded by winter rains, surging rivers carry fallen trees, scrubbed clean of their branches, out of the forest and into the ocean. The trunks eventually come ashore in the coves, piled by waves into tangles that achieve a structural balance. Studying these beached logs gave Bowman an idea for the house. Given its location, the house had to be able to withstand 90-mph winds. Why not fashion a

structure of native logs into an exposed system of braces that could buttress the house against those winds? This idea led to a tree-trunk exoskeleton of posts, cantilevered beams and buttresses that support the house and brace it against the elements (see the photo below).

The house sits on a triangular flat, sheared off the finger of a small ridge that drops 50 ft. to the beach. The westward corner of the triangle points out to sea, bisecting a 180° coastal view. Bowman flipped through various floor-plan ideas, studying how they might best embrace these views. The plan finally came down to a simple reduction of the site's shape: a right-triangle floor plan pointing out to sea, with glass walls facing northwest and southwest (see the floor plan on the facing page).

The bow points out to sea. On a wild stretch of Oregon coastline, this weekend retreat stands braced against the frequent storms by cedar logs from the local forest.

THE PLAN POINTS WEST

Taking its cue from the shape of the site and direction of the views, the triangular plan allows generous windows facing both up and down the coast. Bedrooms are at opposite ends of the house, tucked behind pocket doors that recede into cavities behind the bookcases.

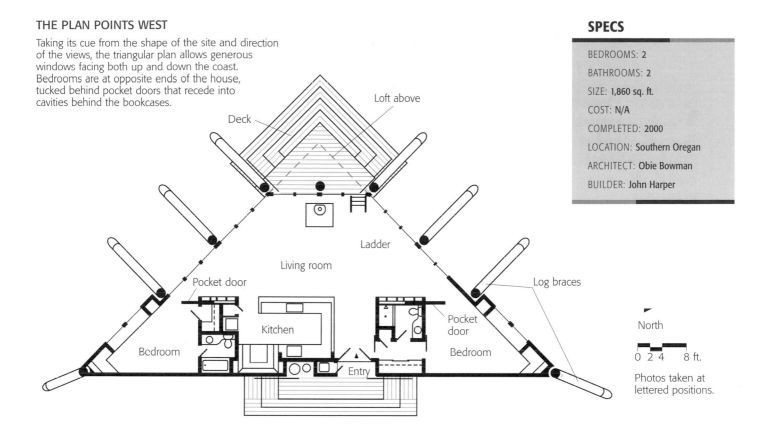

Deck

Loft above

Ladder

Living room

Pocket door

Log braces

Pocket door

Kitchen

Bedroom

Bedroom

Entry

North

0 2 4   8 ft.

Photos taken at lettered positions.

SPECS

BEDROOMS: 2
BATHROOMS: 2
SIZE: 1,860 sq. ft.
COST: N/A
COMPLETED: 2000
LOCATION: Southern Oregan
ARCHITECT: Obie Bowman
BUILDER: John Harper

The plan finally came down to a simple reduction of the site's shape: a right-triangle floor plan pointing out to sea . . .

Entered from the east side, where the roof comes to its lowest point, the house progresses from a sense of shelter to one of almost complete exposure (see the photo above). The view dominates the west side of the house, which culminates in a loft that reaches toward the water. This loft is the perfect place to sip hot coffee and watch the waves as one of Oregon's 90-mph rainstorms slams the coast. Outside, the loft shelters the ocean-side entry.

Balancing the expansive living room, with its tall windows and high ceiling, are the bedrooms and the kitchen (see the photo on the facing page). The two bedroom suites are politely placed at opposite

Entered from the east side, where the roof comes to its lowest point, the house progresses from a sense of shelter to one of almost complete exposure.

The entry is on the lee side. Flanked by the garage, a buttressed fence and the hill in the foreground, the entry courtyard is protected from the prevailing winds. A row of plant shelves leads to a deck atop the garage. Photo taken at C on floor plan.

The kitchen and bedrooms are tucked along the east wall, where the lower ceiling imparts a sense of enclosure Photo taken at F on floor plan.

Great Idea: Stained Concrete Pocket Doors

Concrete came out of the garage and took up residence in the house during the '90s. It arrived as pigmented concrete floors, polished concrete countertops and textured-concrete fireplace surrounds—massive pieces that say: I'm not fake. I'm heavy, I'm solid. Architect Obie Bowman, on the other hand, has found a way to make concrete light, almost translucent. And most of the ingredients he uses are commonly found at home centers.

The big pocket doors that close off the bedrooms from the main room are composed of a steel frame filled with ¼-in.-thick Hardibacker panels. The panels, which are typically used as tile underlayment (see sources on p. 42), were turned into color-field paintings by project architect James Jorgensen (see the photo at right).

Jorgensen spread out the panels on the bluff, wet them down and then applied a thin (15:1) wash of Mission Tan pigment (see sources). While they were still wet, he sprinkled spoonfuls of Miracle-Gro plant food on the panels in random patterns, followed by a scattering of Ironite pellets the size of BBs (see sources). As the fertilizers and pigments dissolved, they spread across the panels as blooms of brick red and coppery green. When the panels dried, the colors remained as integral stains. Builder John Harper finished them with a couple of coats of water-based satin-urethane varnish. —*C. M.*

ends of the house in the remaining points of the triangle. Tall steel-frame pocket doors close off the bedrooms from the main space. The doors have colorful panels made of a common material treated in an uncommon manner (see the sidebar above).

Getting the Logs into the House

John Harper remembers the first time he saw the plans for this house. In his 35 years as a builder, the closest he'd come to constructing a scribe-fit log-buttressed house was a stick-frame ranch with fake-log siding.

But like other builders who are drawn toward creating the unfamiliar, he couldn't resist. He put in a bid to build the house and put out the call for some good local logs.

Centuries ago, Spanish sailors stopped along this part of the Oregon coastline to fix their ships. They were seeking a specific kind of wood: Port Orford cedar, prized for its strength and rot resistance. Taking advantage of this resource, Harper bought several truckloads of Port Orford cedar logs and graded them for size. The 16-in.- to 24-in.-dia. logs were set aside for the frame.

High windows in the west. The ceiling and windows rise as they move toward the view, culminating in the loft. Photo taken at E on floor plan.

SOURCES

L. M. Scofield pigments
800-800-9900
www.scofield.com

Miracle-Gro
800-645-8166
www.miracle-gro.com

**James Hardie Co.
tile underlayment**
888-542-7343
www.jameshardie.com

Ironite
800-677-9941
www.ironite.com

Custom-made steel plates within the logs hold these corners together securely.

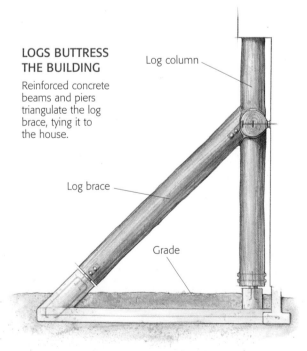

LOGS BUTTRESS THE BUILDING

Reinforced concrete beams and piers triangulate the log brace, tying it to the house.

Log column

Log brace

Grade

The others were cut into 1x boards and stacked in the garage to dry.

The log buttresses do brace the house against the winds, and tying them into the foundation and the log columns that carry the roof was by far the toughest part of building this house. At wall intersections, four logs come together in a carefully fitted assembly (see the photo above). There, they are bolted to one another by way of custom-made ⅜-in. thick steel plates concealed within the logs.

To get them to fit, Harper had to hang each buttress from his boom truck, get it close to position, mark it for scribing, remove it, chainsaw it, put it back, brace it from below at the correct angle and repeat until snug. In this manner, Harper worked

his way around the house, supporting the buttresses from below and letting them run long so that they could be lopped off in line with one another. Then he still wasn't done.

At the ground, each buttress is bolted to a cylindrical concrete pier connecting to a concrete beam that reaches out from the house's foundation (see the drawing on the facing page). Each cylindrical pier was cast in place in cardboard forms wrapped with steel tape to keep them from deforming in their angled state.

By the time the log work was done and the house enclosed, the dehumidifier in the garage had done its work. The stacks of 1x cedar were dry enough to find their way into the house as paneling, cabinets, decking and trim. Outside, the cedar boards are arranged as horizontal siding boards over battens affixed to an exterior plywood shell.

A couple of years have passed since John Harper finished this house. He's still got a trunk full of 24-in. ship-auger bits that he wore out boring holes for the buttress bolts. They're one more reminder of the unforeseeable details that rode in with this project. But as he points out, he has built a lot of houses, and this is the one that people are still talking about. And yes, he's still in business.

Charles Miller is the editor of *Houses*.

Blend lifesaving-station architecture with a touch of Japanese and high Victorian, and you get a stunning cottage with an attached kayak garage.

Block Island Boat House

I N THE SUMMER OF 1993, A CLIENT ASKED ME TO DESIGN a small cottage that would double as a boat house on Block Island, Rhode Island. He set two conditions. The first was that I keep the budget under $100,000, and the second was that I not make an architectural "statement." Aside from screwing up both conditions, I think the building turned out all right.

A Site to Die For

The site for this boat house is a spectacular 60-acre waterfront lot on the northwest end of the island, with views of the landmark North Lighthouse. The adjacent properties are held in conservancy, so there are few structures anywhere in sight. The house was to be built within the footprint of a small building that was falling down.

After tearing down that building, we were left with a site that overlooked a brackish pond separated from the beach and the ocean by some barrier dunes. During the construction of the cottage, we were privy to an incredible display of nature, including bald eagles, snapping turtles feeding on seagulls and an occasional whale. It was sort of like building a house in the middle of Mutual of Omaha's Wild Kingdom, only we never saw Marlin Perkins.

VARIATIONS ON A LIFESAVING THEME

Starting with the basic layout of a historic Coast Guard lifesaving station, the great room was extended to take advantage of magnificent views of the nearby ocean and coastal wildlife, while a garage with doors at both ends was added for storage of kayaks and small boats. The shaded area indicates a sleeping loft over the kitchen.

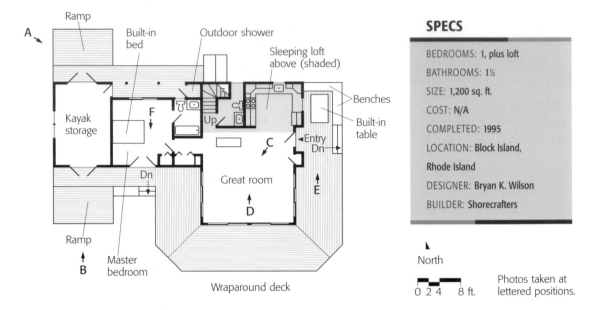

Ramp

A

Built-in bed

Outdoor shower

Sleeping loft above (shaded)

Kayak storage

F

Up

Benches

Built-in table

Entry Dn

C

Great room

D

E

Dn

Dn

Ramp

B

Master bedroom

Wraparound deck

North

0 2 4 8 ft.

Photos taken at lettered positions.

SPECS

BEDROOMS: 1, plus loft

BATHROOMS: 1½

SIZE: 1,200 sq. ft.

COST: N/A

COMPLETED: 1995

LOCATION: Block Island, Rhode Island

DESIGNER: Bryan K. Wilson

BUILDER: Shorecrafters

As the design evolved, I included an eclectic mix of architectural influences.

Lifesaving inspiration. The Coast Guard station inspired the design of the Block Island cottage.

A Lifesaving Station Serves as Inspiration

The program for the house was simple, calling for a kayak-storage room, a living room, a kitchen, 1½ bathrooms and a master bedroom (see the floor plan above). I took the basic design of the house from a Bibbs #2 lifesaving station, an example of which still exists on the island today, having been con-

verted into a residence. The #2 (see the photo at left) was one of several buildings designed by Albert B. Bibbs that stood watch over this country's coastlines from the early 1800s until the 1920s.

As the design evolved, I included an eclectic mix of architectural influences. I have always admired how traditional Japanese architecture integrates interior spaces with the surrounding environment. With this in mind, I pulled the living room from the main body of the building with large glass doors on three sides. The result: The living room is surrounded on three sides by the beauty of the site (see the bottom photo on the facing page).

As the design for the living room unfolded, the room began to take on other features reminiscent of lifesaving-station great rooms. In a typical station, this room served as boat storage and mess hall as well as being a general gathering place. In this house, the great room includes the kitchen and an informal sitting and eating area (see the top photo on the facing page) with a sleeping loft

For the ceilings in every room, we used pine beadboard stained red to mimic that rich well-worn hue.

As an echo of the interior treatment in a historic Block Island lodge, pine beadboard with a rich patina wraps the sleeping loft above the kitchen and informal eating area. Photo taken at D on floor plan.

Gathering places inside and out. With large glass doors on three walls, the living room projects from the main body of the house surrounded by the natural beauty of the site. Photo taken at C on floor plan.

When prevailing sea breezes allow, guests can share meals at this outdoor dining area with table and benches built into the wraparound deck. Photo taken at E on floor plan.

Interior Finish with the Flavor of an Island Lodge

Another important influence on the design is the Victorian architectural legacy of Block Island, in particular the Sullivan House, originally known as the Ninigret Lodge. The interior of this building is finished with horizontal yellow-pine beadboard that has acquired a deep patina.

For the ceilings in every room, we used pine beadboard stained red to mimic that rich well-worn hue. Where the ceilings are vaulted in the master bedroom and the great room, beadboard was also applied to the interior gable walls. The walls below the beadboard were kept white to allow as much reflection of ambient light as possible and to help focus attention on the outside vistas.

The beadboard theme was continued in the custom furniture designed and built by Tom Holburton, a local craftsman. In the master bedroom, the headboard is done in vertical oak beadboard with a gently arched top echoing the arch-top French doors that open toward the water. Vanities in the bathrooms were also given a beadboard treatment, and in the great room, the informal eating bar was finished in beadboard as well.

Designer Picks up a Hammer

After finalizing the design of the boat house, we spent the following year navigating a somewhat tortuous permitting process because the site was located in an environmentally sensitive area. By the fall of 1994, everything was in place to begin construction.

The contractor for the boat house (see the photo on the facing page) was Shorecrafters, an island firm headed by Bob Closter. As it happened, I was working for

above. The great room extends outdoors onto a wraparound deck with a built-in eating area at one end (see the photo above).

To give the great room a more spacious feel, I gave the modified Dutch-hip roof a fairly steep pitch (18-in-12). The steep roof also ensured that headroom would not be a problem in the loft. To break up the exterior roof planes and to add light to the interior, I added a dormer and placed a cupola on the peak. A lamp suspended in the cupola makes it look like a lantern at night.

Park your kayak here. A garage on the north end of the boat house serves as storage for various watercraft that can be used in the ocean or in the nearby brackish pond. Photo taken at B on floor plan.

Shorecrafters as a carpenter at the time, which allowed us to delve into the much-debated realm of design/build.

The primary advantage of the design/build approach, other than the practical experience that it brings to the designer, is the fluidity it lends to the building process. Throughout construction, the design was re-evaluated, altered and improved. Many of the refinements in this building were the result of on-site discussions among Bob Closter, the clients, and me, along with the subcontractors and even the occasional pedestrian.

Bryan K. Wilson designs and builds houses on Block Island, RI.

A House Shaped by Its Site

W HEN DREW THORBURN UNCOVERED THE SKULL,
it looked so fresh that he feared the worst and phoned the
police. But later, when they uncovered the whole skeleton,
lying in the fetal position barely 8 in. below the ground, consultation with
the local Saanich Indians and with the archaeologists at Simon Fraiser
University revealed that Lucy, as the skeleton came to be known, was at
least 900 years old.

Public spaces face the view. This house sits on a hill that slopes from north to south. So the house steps down the hill, but the ridgeline remains level, which means that the cathedral-ceilinged rooms inside grow taller as you move toward the dining area and living room. These public spaces also enjoy the panoramic water view to the south.

Lucy was found on Isabella Point, a south-facing hillside that slopes gently toward the sea and forms the southern tip of Saltspring Island on British Columbia's lower Gulf of Georgia. With plenty of sunshine and fresh water, ample beaches and commanding views of the local waterways and islands, Isabella Point has been witness to centuries of habitation, first by the Saanich and later by Hawaiian immigrants.

Drew and Lynn Thorburn and their family had lived in an old farmhouse at Isabella Point on and off for over 20 years. When they decided to build a new home, they knew where they wanted the house to go, pretty well what rooms it should have and even where some of those rooms should be. But they really didn't have an idea of what their new home

The roofline follows the hillside. Inspired by the gentle contours of the land, the eaves on this house curve, climb and dive as they make their way around the building. On the south elevation (shown here), the roofline rises to its highest peak, making room for a wall of glass. Photo taken at B on floor plan.

Every site has its own personality and character. And part of that character is an inherent geometry.

might look like in the end. Clearly, though, it would have to be a special house to suit this beautiful, historic site.

Balancing the Desires of the Clients with the Demands of the Site

On the day I first visited Drew and Lynn, they took me for a tour of their property and told me some of their dreams for the new house. In recent years, Drew had taken a keen interest in timber-framing and wanted their new home to be a timber frame. Lynn is an avid horsewoman with ambi-

tious, well-established gardens. There were 250 chickens in the yard, gum boots, rain gear, and dog beds on the porch of the old farmhouse. Their lifestyle was more than superficially rural.

Drew and Lynn's program was not unusual: open living areas with a den for Drew, a bedroom suite and guest room, and easy access to lots of outdoor living space. They would need a serious mudroom with space for everything from dogs to saddles. It would become the main traffic area for the family.

People don't hire me to design colonials, ranches or bungalows; I'm just not a gable-roof-and-chimney kind of guy. I've spent the past 25 years learning to design houses that are integrated with the landscape.

For me the process of design is one of discovery, of asking questions and listening. Every site has its own personality and character. And part of that character is an inherent geometry. It's important to discover that geometry and to develop a feeling for the character of the site.

There's not a lot of mystery to the process, really. It can be as simple as noticing where the sun rises and sets, the slope of the land, the views and the weather patterns. If you pay attention, the results can be quite surprising.

Compass, Tape Measure and Video Camera Aid Site Analysis

After touring the property with Drew and Lynn and spending some time at the house site, I was left on my own for a while. I staked out the main sight line, which looked south over a large group of broadleaf maples. I measured the site, taking compass bearings to record critical views and features. I've found it helpful to use a video camera as a visual notebook. I use an inclinometer to get the basic slopes of the land.

Drew and Lynn had chosen an interesting location for their house (see the photo on the facing page), well clear of the archaeologically sensitive areas. The site is the confluence of several natural features: where the upper forest gives way to the gentler slopes of the fields, amid a group of maples on the east, a large cedar on the northwest corner and a magnificent arbutus tree on the northeast. To the southeast, the land falls toward the beach and the lower garden area. Lynn wanted the kitchen to be on the east side looking toward the sunrise, the San Juan Islands and Mount Baker.

As I became familiar with the site, an image began to take shape in my mind. I imagined a gently undulating sod roof—much like the meadow itself—placed at the edge of the forest, sheltering a series of spaces whose floors would step down with the slope.

The views to the south from the house site are divided by the maples in the distance. We could let this natural feature focus the organization of the house, form-

With the floors stepping down the site, the spaces would open up into the social parts of the house.

The entrance hall bisects the house. Forming the spine of the house, the entrance hall is lit by skylights in an arched roof. As the hall moves toward the living room, the floor steps down, but the ceiling doesn't, which leads to tall spaces and grand views in the public parts of the house. Photo taken at C on floor plan.

SPECS

BEDROOMS: **2**

BATHROOMS: **2½**

HEATING SYSTEM: **Ground-source heat pump**

SIZE: **3,500 sq. ft.**

COST: **$205.00 per sq. ft. (Canadian)**

COMPLETED: **1994**

LOCATION: **Saltspring Island, B.C. Canada**

North

0 2 4   8 ft.

Photos taken at lettered positions.

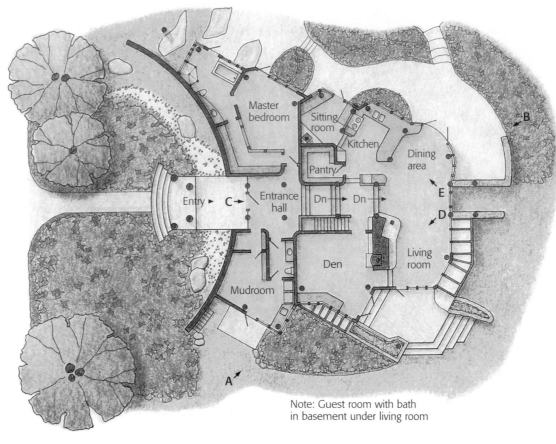

Note: Guest room with bath in basement under living room

ing an axial entrance hall (see the photo on p. 53) with rooms off each side stepping down with the slope. The mudroom needed to be near the main entrance and on the west side to give access to the rest of the farm. The bedroom suite would be on the east side, protected from the entry but open to the southeast views and the arbutus tree on that side.

As I imagined the house, you could approach the entrance from the uphill side and see right over the roof to the views beyond. With the floors stepping down the site, the spaces would open up into the social parts of the house (kitchen, dining area, living room), and we could use the different view orientations to give the rooms individual character.

I worked out the basic room positions in a kind of to-scale bubble diagram on a freehand site plan that showed major features

with compass bearings and distances, and checked it out with Drew and Lynn. Then I returned home to sit down with the site measurements and more formal drawing tools to develop the floor plan and the roof shape (see the floor plan above).

Site-Inspired Design Makes for Some Construction Challenges

The concept of a gently undulating roof shape is one thing. The reality of building a timber frame that has several different floor levels—and over 50 rafters, each with a different slope—is another matter. Drew put together the building team, and the timber framers from the Cascade Joinery were brought to the project at an early stage. They worked closely with me and with the engineer, Josef Novacek, to size and detail the frame (see the sidebar on pp. 56–57).

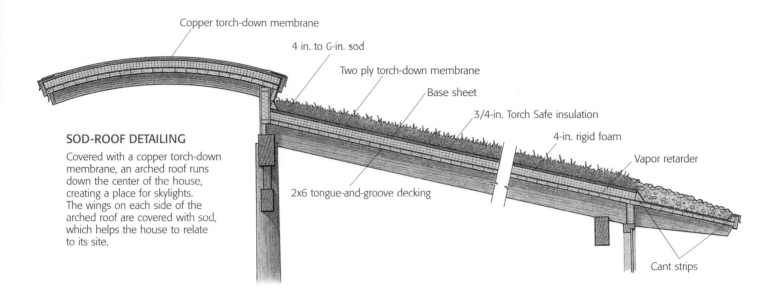

Copper torch-down membrane

4 in. to 6-in. sod

Two ply torch-down membrane

Base sheet

3/4-in. Torch Safe insulation

4-in. rigid foam

Vapor retarder

SOD-ROOF DETAILING

Covered with a copper torch-down membrane, an arched roof runs down the center of the house, creating a place for skylights. The wings on each side of the arched roof are covered with sod, which helps the house to relate to its site.

2x6 tongue-and-groove decking

Cant strips

Once approvals were obtained, my friend Alan Fletcher and his crew from Pacific Wind Construction started building the foundations and floor platforms while Cascade Joinery worked on the timber frame in their shop.

Everything came together one week in August at the timber raising. I was nervous when it was time to set rafters; we would soon know just how this event was going to unfold.

The timber-frame crew started with one of the most extreme rafters, just to see how well our careful calculations had worked out. Up went the rafter on the crane sling, over and down into position. It fit perfectly. Rafter after rafter was lifted, swung and set down without a hitch. Once the timber frame was erected, the space of the house could be felt and appreciated. And the form could be seen from the outside.

After the timber raising, the next step was to install the roof system and to frame the interior and exterior walls. The roof has 2x6 spruce tongue-and-groove decking over the rafters, forming the ceilings and soffits (see the drawing above). The decking is

topped with a vapor-barrier membrane, 4 in. of high-density foam insulation, rigid-fiberglass board and a torch-down membrane. The main roof is covered by a 4-in. to 6-in. layer of sod. The entrance-hall roof, which forms the spine of the house, is topped with copper-faced torch down (see sources on p. 59). By holding the insulation back at the wall line, we could use a much smaller fascia, which has to cover only the edge of the decking and a cant strip.

Interior Finishes also Reflect the Site

The timber frame is designed to stand free of the exterior walls, allowing them to become true curtain walls and allowing the glazing to be free of the frame. The structure is braced by interior shear walls. From most vantage points inside, the windows disappear behind beams on their way to the ceiling (see the photo on p. 58), giving a light appearance to an otherwise heavy assemblage.

When the goal is to build a house that becomes part of the landscape, a chrome

Fifty Rafters, No Two Alike

Timber-frame buildings are normally orderly affairs. All square and level. Either architect Michael McNamara didn't know this, or his sense of order inclines more toward chaos than normal.

The first quick look at his design for the Thorburn residence revealed that the plates weren't level, that rafters intersected some plates at 90° and others at 30°, and that the eave line actually undulated (see the drawing at right). The project had all the appearances of another whacked-out piece of hippie architecture. But as hard as it may be to admit, after only a little study, the sense of the plan revealed itself, not only as sound but also as one that would offer our timber-framing company some worthy challenges.

A Spreadsheet Program Calculates the Angles

The first challenge was to find a mathematical description of an undulating roof. Michael had established column locations and plate heights to create the desired amount of undulation, so calculating rise-and-run coordinates for each intersection of plate and rafter was simple but tedious, because each of the 50-plus rafters in the frame had its own pitch.

The trickier calculation was that of the side-cut, or top, angle (the angle at which the rafter crosses the plate when adjusted for pitch). This angle would be needed on both ends of each rafter and on all the bird's mouths. If anyone is interested, the formula is something like this: The tangent of the side-cut angle is the square root of the sum of rise squared and run squared divided by the run times the square root of three. An electronic spreadsheet helped with these calculations.

A Router Cuts the Bird's Mouths

The rafter-to-plate connections were simple in concept: bird's mouth notches in the 6x10 rafters with lag bolts attaching them to the plates. But because the plates weren't level and because the rafters crossed the plates at an irregular angle (as seen in the plan view), the notches were compound angles.

Using the side-cut angles we had calculated, we located the heel cut of the bird's mouth. Then, working with a "theoretical height above plate" at the centerline of the rafter, we calculated the rise of the plate as it passed under the rafter. Level lines from those points completed the layout of the bird's-mouth notch.

We seem unable to pass up an opportunity to use a router, so after making the heel cut with a circular saw set for the shallowest part of the cut, we screwed guide boards to the side of the rafters parallel with and a prescribed distance above the level lines (see the detail drawing at right). Then it was a simple matter of running a router with a top-bearing bit and an extended base back and forth across the timber between the guide boards to create the seat cut, freehanding close to the heel cut. A little cleanup with a chisel completed the notch.

When a Plan Comes Together

Neat-and-tidy timber frames are fairly easy to assemble because they are more or less self-aligning. If you're off a bit, the connecting beams usually will bring the frame into alignment.

On this project there weren't many connecting beams, so the post-and-beam assemblies running at a 30° angle to the central "spine" would have to be set with exceptional accuracy, which in turn required that the full-scale layout of the posts on the deck be dead on. With some of the lines of posts running over 80 ft. and with the posts required to sit on rebar pins, the job required well-focused minds.

After the prep work, the raising was largely uneventful for us. But as Michael watched the first of the rafters settle into place, he turned and said, "It fits!" For some reason, he seemed genuinely surprised.

—Jeff Arvin and his partner, Craig Aument, run The Cascade Joinery in Everson, Washington. A more in-depth article about the framing of this project appeared in the September 1996 issue of Timber Framing: The Journal of the Timber-Framers Guild *(360-733-4001).*

An Undulating Roof

Conceptually, this house has a central spine and a pair of undulating wings. To create the undulations, the front walls of the house slope and curve; elsewhere, the beams that carry the rafters also slope, and the rafters continually vary in length and pitch.

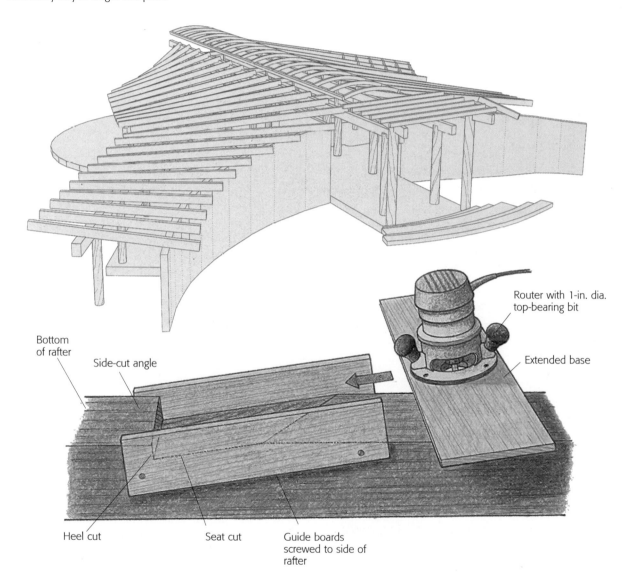

Bottom of rafter

Side-cut angle

Router with 1-in. dia. top-bearing bit

Extended base

Heel cut

Seat cut

Guide boards screwed to side of rafter

Exterior walls don't support the roof. The peeled logs that carry this roof stand inside the building envelope. Their treelike presence inside the house means that no headers are needed in the exterior wall; hence, the windows can run nearly to the ceiling. Photo taken at E on floor plan.

Local sandstone is a focal point inside. The fireplace was built by Derek Lundy, who works an old quarry on Saltspring Island that's accessible only by boat. He loaded the stone by hand onto a barge and delivered it to the site, where he cut each piece to create the randomly coursed sculpture at the center of the house. Photo taken at D on floor plan.

and vinyl interior won't do. We chose interior materials from a natural palette: Ceilings, of course, are wood, floors are either maple or slate, kitchen counters are granite, and the fireplace (see the photo above) was built of local sandstone from an old quarry on Saltspring.

Drew and Lynn have lived in the house for a couple of years now and seem happy with the place. It's a house that's comfortable with dogs, kids and muddy boots, but where fine meals and single malt scotches are equally at home.

For me, the greatest pleasure is riding the ferry into Fulford Harbor and trying to see the house, but from most vantage points on the water, it almost disappears into the beauty of the point. If you're trying to point it out to someone, you have to say, "See the old farmhouse there, the one with the red roof? . . . Well, it's just to the right, by the edge of the trees."

Michael McNamara is a founding partner of Blue Sky Design, a design/build firm. He has been doing architectural design from Hornby Island, B.C. since the early 1970s.

SOURCES

Sopralene Flam Copper, Soprema Inc.,
Quebec, Canada G1N 1C9
418-681-8127
www.sopremaworld.com

Mango House

HURRICANE HUGO SLAMMED INTO THE ISLAND OF ST. CROIX at dusk on Sept. 17, 1989. In the 12 hours that followed, Hugo thrashed its way along the spine of the island, traveling the 23 miles from east to west at a tortuous 2 mph. Hugo was a Category-5 hurricane, with sustained winds in excess of 150 mph, and the backside of the storm carried a cluster of tornadoes whose winds were estimated at 250 mph. No building on the island survived undamaged.

St. Croix, in fact, was devastated. The island had been green with tropical plants before Hugo; in its wake was a brown wasteland. Most buildings on the island were severely damaged. Many were destroyed. One of these badly damaged buildings was a single-story, three-unit dwelling in the hills overlooking Christiansted. The building was next to a house I had designed a few years earlier for Elizabeth and Michael Kaiser. After Hugo, the Kaisers acquired the wrecked building and asked me to design a three-bedroom guest house on the same foundation.

A major part of my job was to design a house that took advantage of the climatic conditions on St. Croix. To keep the house comfortable, natural cross ventilation was used, rather than an elaborate mechanical cooling system. The wood-framed second story includes 6-ft.-wide roof overhangs to shield the walls and the windows from sunlight (see the photo on the facing page). And the new building is anchored solidly to the concrete slab and existing concrete-block walls so that the house would better resist storms like Hugo that might strike in the future.

Shade in the tropics. Roof overhangs of more than 6 ft. help screen exterior walls and windows from intense Caribbean sunlight. Rainwater collected from the galvanized steel roof is piped to a cistern for use later. Photo taken at A on floor plan.

Using What Hugo Left

Most of the demolition on the existing structure had been done by the storm. The flat, wooden roof and all the windows had been not-so-neatly removed by Hugo, leaving the concrete slab and reinforced concrete-block bearing walls capped by steel-reinforced concrete bond beams. It was my intent to use as much of the remaining masonry and concrete structure as I could. The original 51-ft. by 28-ft. building was divided into four bays, each about 12-ft. wide, by concrete-block bearing walls. I decided that portions of the two middle walls should be removed to open up the first-floor living area. To complete the demolition, several interior non-load-bearing partitions were removed.

The remaining wall configuration provided an open first-floor plan that accommodates an entry foyer and a powder room, the living and dining areas, a kitchen and a library/bedroom with bath (see the floor plan at left). I maintained an existing 1-ft. level change in the floor slab but changed its location slightly to separate kitchen and foyer spaces from the adjacent living areas. The exterior walkway on the west side (the entry side) of the building made a perfect entry veranda when covered by a broad roof overhang. Beyond the kitchen is a covered deck leading to a swimming pool (see the photo on the facing page). On the second floor, two more bedrooms, each with a bath, were placed above the remaining bearing walls of the north and south bays. This plan left the two center bays (a total of about 25 ft.) open with a two-story living room between them. A wooden bridge, partially supported by 3/8-in. steel tension rods hung from the roof, connects the two bedrooms and provides access to a stair.

It all worked on paper, but making this design a reality on an island 1,100 miles southeast of Miami, Florida, had its complications. When my architectural firm designed the Kaisers' main house a few years earlier, Michael and I experienced two problems: We never seemed to have the materials on site when we needed them, and there weren't enough skilled craftsmen working on the house every day. In taking on the new guest house, we were determined to

First floor

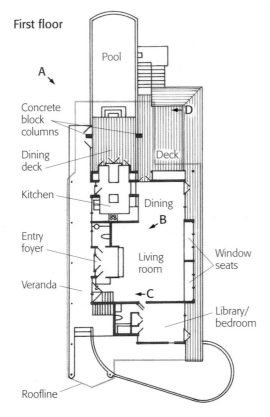

Pool

A

Concrete block columns

Dining deck

Kitchen

Entry foyer

Veranda

Roofline

D

Deck

Dining

B

Living room

Window seats

C

Library/ bedroom

Second floor

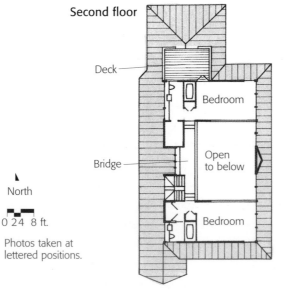

Deck

Bedroom

Bridge

Open to below

Bedroom

North

0 2 4 8 ft.

Photos taken at lettered positions.

A deck for dining. Beyond the kitchen is a pool and a covered dining deck. The structure is supported by concrete columns and bond beams reinforced with steel. Photo taken at D on floor plan.

avoid these pitfalls. My firm calculated the materials needed and ordered supplies from the states early enough to ensure a timely arrival on the site. Michael recruited quality craftsmen who were committed for the duration of the project.

As it happened, Michael was overseeing the restoration of his 19th-century house in Palm Beach, Florida, just as I was beginning to design the guest house. Working on the Florida job were three Finnish carpenters in their 50s, and Michael asked them if they would build the guest house in St. Croix when their work in Florida was complete. They agreed, and I began design work confident that the house would be built skillfully.

The carpenters were supervised by Torsti Laine, one of the Finns from Florida. The design included an upper story with an exposed timber frame and other wood architectural details, so their superb carpentry skills were critical to our success.

Cooling in the Tropics

Big storms aside, the island's climate is as predictable as it is pleasant: 15-mph trade winds that blow almost constantly from the east, 12-hour exposures to cloudless solar radiation, a temperature range of between 62° and 94° and annual rainfall of 45 in. Natural cross ventilation is the ideal method for making houses comfortable in

Caribbean roofs not only serve the traditional purposes of providing shade, insulation and shelter from rain, but they also provide surface area to catch potable water.

Second-floor bridge. The two bedrooms on the second floor are linked by a bridge spanning the 25-ft. living room below. Photo taken at B on floor plan.

The ash plywood with cypress base and vertical battens became the interior finish on the second floor.

the tropics. The 360-day dependability of the trade winds allowed us to provide operable windows on windward and leeward sides to control the natural airflow through all rooms and obviate the need for mechanical systems. I did, however, include large ceiling fans in each room to aid ventilation on those rare windless days. The open, two-story plan of the house, with its rooms overlooking and interconnected with one another, further enhances the natural ventilation by introducing a chimney effect. Hot air rises two stories to a large exhaust

dormer that removes the hottest air at roof level and induces cooler air to enter at the lower living levels.

Having introduced windows for ventilation and views, I added broad roof overhangs to protect them, as well as the exterior walls, from direct sunlight during the hottest part of the day. The second line of defense against the hot sun was insulation: 5½ in. of fiberglass batt insulation in the second-story walls and 2½ in. of rigid foam insulation in the roof. The foam insulation installed on top of the 1x6 T&G roof sheathing stops the heat, and the roof structure—some of the best craftsmanship of the Finnish carpenters—is open to view from the rooms below. Rooms that produce heat or odors, like the kitchen and the bathrooms, are located next to the leeward wall to provide a direct and natural exhaust.

Another climatic factor is rainfall, an important consideration in residential design on St. Croix. Caribbean roofs not only serve the traditional purposes of providing shade, insulation and shelter from rain, but they also provide surface area to catch potable water. The guest house, which the owners call Mango House, relies on a cistern that stores rain for its only source of water. Most houses on the island have similar arrangements.

Timber Frame Above

To make the best use of the carpenters' skills and to limit any additional load on the existing foundation, I designed the second floor to be of timber-frame construction instead of masonry. I thought that having a one-story masonry separation between the wood of the second floor and the voracious local termites would be enough. This, however, turned out to be another Northeastern practice that was not applicable to the Caribbean. Through research it became apparent that, in at least one stage of their lives, Caribbean termites fly. So having one story of concrete between wood and the ground didn't offer enough protection. My thoughts of building an exposed timber frame started fading to a pale shade of green as I visualized lumber treated with chromated copper arsenate (CCA).

My search for an effective alternative to CCA-treated wood led to the U. S. Forest Service experimental station in Gulfport, Mississippi, which had been testing a borate treatment for wood (see the sidebar at right). One of the best features of this alter-

native to CCA treatment is that borate doesn't change the natural color of the wood. With the design work complete and construction documents in hand, the entire lumber list was established, cut in South

Borate: The CCA Alternative

The construction of the guest house on St. Croix called for the use of treated wood to guard against the Formosan termites that are so prevalent on Caribbean islands. I wanted to expose timbers and roof sheathing, but the pale-green hues of wood treated with chromated copper arsenate (CCA) seemed inappropriate. The alternative was lumber treated with sodium borate, which is extracted from borax ore. The ore is mined in California's Mojave Desert.

Borate treatment has been used for 50 years in New Zealand, Australia and England to discourage decay and insect damage in building materials. Water-soluble sodium borate is introduced into the wood in one of two ways: either through dip diffusion for green wood or by conventional vacuum-pressure treatment for kiln-dried wood. In dip diffusion, freshly cut lumber is lowered into a vat of the borate solution where it soaks for a few minutes. The wood is then air dried for four to eight weeks. During this period the borate migrates through the wood, penetrating even the heartwood. The borate solution can even be sprayed on wood already in place as a remedial treatment for insect infestation or fungus, although this method is not nearly as effective.

U. S. Borax, Inc. sells the material used in the process and licenses companies to sell treated lumber under the Tim-Bor and Cari-Bor trademarks (see sources on 67). Borate treatment does not affect the natural color of the wood, but it makes the wood toxic to insects and fungus. According to the company, the process eliminates harsh chemical treatments that might pose a danger to building occupants or to tradesmen. In addition, borate treatment doesn't change the workability of the wood; it increases the wood's resistance to flames; and it isn't corrosive to metal fasteners. Treatment is relatively inexpensive.

A disadvantage of the borate treatment is that the borate solution remains water soluble. As a result, borate-treated wood is not recommended for applications where it will be submerged in water or placed in contact with the ground. Nor would it be recommended for installation next to masonry surfaces, as a mudsill would be. According to U. S. Borax, however, the application of a water-repellent finish (like a paint or a wood sealer) over the borate-treated wood allows it to be used in some exterior applications. The company also is trying to figure out how to fix the borate in the wood during treatment. —P. M.

Carolina, treated with borate in Savannah, Georgia, and shipped to the job site, all within two months. Because borate-treated lumber was a little more expensive than CCA-treated wood and not as resistant to weather, I opted for borate-treated lumber only where it would be exposed. In most other applications, and especially where the lumber would be in contact with concrete or exposed to the weather, CCA-treated lumber was used.

Key structural elements of the second-story are 6x6 timber columns that were anchored either to the existing concrete bond beam at the top of the first-story block walls or to the first-floor slab with prefabricated steel hold-downs and expansion bolts. The columns support the roof and provide resistance against lifting forces in high winds. To make a smooth transition from the 8-in. concrete-block walls of the

Framing details. Roof overhangs are supported by eaves beams and diagonal braces.

first floor, the second floor was framed with 2x8s up to the level of the windowsills. Above that, walls are of 2x6 construction. The difference in the width of the outside wall created a 2-in. ledge where we installed a pitched water table around the perimeter of the house. The water table was capped with ironwood, a superior weather-resistant species.

Building the Roof

With the timber columns and second-story walls in place, the next step was to build the roof structure. To each 6x6 timber column the carpenters attached a pair of 2x6 diagonal outriggers that reach up to support eaves beams (see the photo at left). The eaves beams are pairs of 2x12s with 2x spacers between them that support the 3x10 southern yellow pine roof rafters. The rafters cross the eaves beams 2 ft. from the outside wall and continue out another 5 ft. to provide about 6 ft. of shade around the building. All timber-to-timber connections were carefully notched and bolted and reinforced with specially fabricated steel splice plates. Wherever windows didn't get in the way, the exterior walls were reinforced with 1½-in.-wide, 12-ga. steel diagonal bracing for increased rigidity and wind resistance.

Between each rafter—sandwiched between the eaves beam below and the roof sheathing above—I selected clear glass panels instead of more conventional frieze blocks. The glass seems to make the 40-ft. by 60-ft. hip roof float above its support system and brings light into what is usually the darkest part of a house—the space where the roof and the wall meet. The glass is held between a pair of 2x2s that are through-bolted to the rafters. The 2xs trap the glass and anchor the rafters to the eaves beams.

The roof over the 25-ft. living room is supported by a parallel-chord truss that acts as a structural ridge beam. The rafters and the decking were planed prior to installation, so no further finish was required. The roof is capped with corrugated steel roofing over the foam insulation and a layer of 15-lb. felt. The galvanized roof panels run from ridge to eaves without horizontal seams. The panels are attached to 2x3 purlins with screws and neoprene washers. I located the galvanized steel gutters about 1 ft. above the ends of the decorative rafter tails and provided drain lines to pipe roof water to the cistern below.

Sheathing and Interior Details

I wanted a stucco finish on the exterior of both the first and second floors, so structural sheathing was installed on the interior of the building. That's the reverse of the usual U. S. standard of applying drywall on the inside surface of exterior walls and plywood on the outside. I selected ½-in. straight-grain ash veneer plywood as the interior finish and shear wall. The plywood is nailed to the studs, and the nail heads are covered with cypress battens (see the photo at right).

The ash plywood with cypress base and vertical battens became the interior finish on the second floor. The wood got a light stain. The ash plywood was set flush with mahogany window and door casings so that the simple trapezoidal battens not only covered the joint between adjacent panels but also joints between panels and doors and panels and windows.

On the first floor, the concrete slab was covered with CCA-treated wood sleepers and 1x6 T&G cypress flooring. CCA-treated floor joists and plywood underlayment created the new bedroom floors on the second

Nice stair, but the balustrade wouldn't meet U. S. codes. Photo taken at C on floor plan.

level, followed by the 1x4 cypress T&G finish floors. Extensive cypress trim, including base and crown molding, ties the part-stucco, part-wood construction of the first floor to the all-wood construction of the second floor. The wide window seats on the first floor, the mahogany door trim and stair treads and the ash-plywood kitchen cabinets are treated with AwlGrip, a two-part polyurethane product that stands up well to abrasion and sunlight (see sources).

Peter Mullen is a partner in Mullen, Palandrani Architects in New York City, NY.

SOURCES

U. S. Paint
314-621-0525
www.uspaint.com

U. S. Borax, Inc.
Valencia, CA
805-287-5463

Guest House by the Bay

A cozy old cabin on the river.
Embedded corner boards and
changing rooflines create the feeling of a little old house that never
stopped growing. A balcony off
the upstairs master bedroom takes
in the view. Photo taken at A on
floor plan.

S CATTERED ALONG THE NORTHERN FINGERS OF CHESAPEAKE
Bay stands a collection of unlikely billboards. They are boathouses built long ago by highly skilled boatbuilders during the
slow winter months. Rustic, even primitive, on the inside yet finely
finished on the outside, these land-bound structures were calling cards,
promoting their builders' skill and craftsmanship to anyone who happened to sail by. That's why it's not unusual to see highly creative trim

elements that have been grafted to these otherwise modest structures.

Several years ago my clients bought an old Maryland dairy farm that included one of these dilapidated old boathouses. They hoped to resurrect the boathouse as a guest house, creating a comfortable place for his mother to stay during her frequent visits, but one that could also be used for large family gatherings. The old structure turned out to be too far gone to save. But its spirit, at least, was reborn in a new body (see the floor plans on p. 72).

Building an Old Boathouse

New construction in the Chesapeake Bay area is prohibited within 1,000 ft. of the waterline at mean high tide. We were permitted to build here because the guest house retained the footprint of the existing

The warmest room in the house. Despite being part of the same great-room floor space that includes the two-story kitchen and dining areas, the area in front of the fireplace is a more intimate, comfortable space on a smaller scale. Photo taken at F on floor plan.

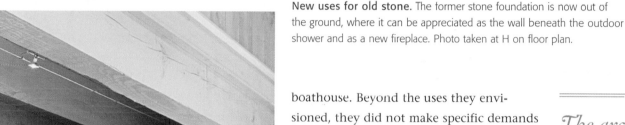

New uses for old stone. The former stone foundation is now out of the ground, where it can be appreciated as the wall beneath the outdoor shower and as a new fireplace. Photo taken at H on floor plan.

boathouse. Beyond the uses they envisioned, they did not make specific demands for a particular style for Little Elk, as they named the guest house. Their only requirements were that the structure not dominate the view of the water from the main house up the hill and that it be sympathetic to its environment and its history.

The architecture of Maryland's Eastern Shore has traditionally reflected its connection to the water. Many of the ancient fishing cabins and boathouses that dot the shoreline have evolved significantly over the years. Oftentimes, families converted the boathouses to residential use, first adding a screened porch, later framing in that porch, then adding a new porch. These houses were my inspiration.

The rooflines and the exterior trim suggest an old house that never stopped growing (see the photo on pp. 68–69). Embedded corner boards extend up the gable-end walls to the point where the roof pitch changes, as if shed-roof additions had been grafted onto each side of a once-tiny house. The roof overhang stops at the "additions" to emphasize this effect. One of the porches is screened (see the photo above), one is open, and one is enclosed, implying that

> *The architecture of Maryland's Eastern Shore has traditionally reflected its connection to the water.*

A COMFY YET EXPANSIVE RETREAT

Although primarily designed to be a cozy guest house for the owner's mother, this small cottage has an open floor plan and large screened porch that let it be the site of large family gatherings at the river.

SPECS

BEDROOMS: 2

BATHROOMS: 2

SIZE: 1,674 sq. ft.

COST: n/a

COMPLETED: 1997

LOCATION: North East, Maryland

ARCHITECT: Peter Zimmerman Architects

BUILDER: Dan Burris (PHB Inc.)

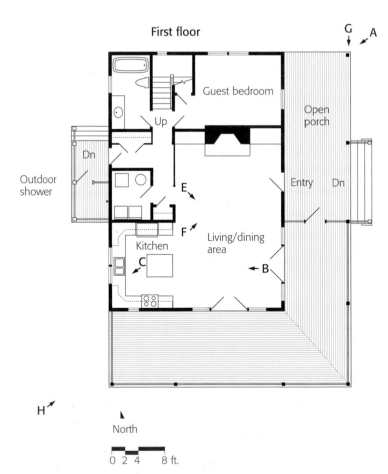

Second floor

Dn

Master bedroom

Balcony

D

Open to below

First floor

G   A

Guest bedroom

Open porch

Up

Dn

Outdoor shower

Entry   Dn

E

Kitchen

F

C

Living/dining area

B

H

North

0 2 4   8 ft.

Photos taken at lettered positions.

each of the house's porches was built at different times.

Historically, the building materials in this area of the country were primarily wood and brick—the brick arrived here as ballast in ships—but this tiny pocket of the Eastern Shore is one of the few areas where you see native stone. We salvaged the stone from the foundation of the old boathouse and used it to face the new foundation and to create the central fireplace (see the photo on p. 70). Indoors and out, we used authentic, salvaged hardware from the late-19th century. All our hardware for the house came from the Michael M. Coldren Company in North East, Maryland (see sources on p. 75). Mike has one of the largest collections of 18th- and 19th-century hardware anywhere in the United States.

A Place for Every Season

Wraparound porches and oversize French doors allow Little Elk to expand for large parties and contract for warmth. In cold weather, with the doors closed, it's intimate and cozy, especially in front of a roaring fire in the stone fireplace. When it's time for the annual summer get-together, both sets of French doors in the dining area fold back on themselves, opening the walls onto the porches and letting in plenty of light and ventilation (see the photo on the facing page and the bottom left photo on p.74). The porches are extra deep, which shields the interior spaces from the hot summer sun.

There's no drywall in the house because a boathouse that was converted to living space would have been roughly paneled with whatever material was at hand. To brighten the interior, the woodwork is

An expansive space for entertaining. When the French doors that separate the dining area from the screened porch are open, the outside walls all but disappear. Photo taken at E on floor plan.

A loft if you want it to be. Drawing back a 6-ft.-wide set of bifold shutters opens the south wall of the master bedroom onto the dining area below. Photo taken at D on floor plan.

There's no drywall in the house because a boathouse that was converted to living space would have been roughly paneled with whatever material was at hand.

Indoor/outdoor dining. Alternative dining spaces flank the alcove kitchen. Photo taken at B on floor plan.

finished with a light stain that allows the knots and natural grain to show through. The baseboards and casings are also finely planed knotty pine that's simply butted but subtly detailed with an occasional beaded edge.

Deep screened porches could make a house feel dark and gloomy inside, so the upper-level windows are designed to funnel sunlight deep into the house. The loftlike master bedroom on the second floor has bifold shutters that open onto the dining area below or close for privacy (see the top photo on the facing page). The master bedroom also has a private balcony, with French doors that open the wall to a view of sky and water.

The Fun Is in the Details

Throughout the planning, we never forgot that the guest house is a place for holidays, parties and fun. As a show of respect for our boat-building predecessors, I threw in a few whimsical details for guests to discover.

Everyone's favorite detail is the rafter tails. My clients changed the farm's livestock from dairy cows to thoroughbred racehorses, so it seemed appropriate to carve the exposed rafter tails to resemble horses stretching for the finish line (see the bottom photo at right).

Local visitors can't help but notice the Chinese Chippendale railing that surrounds the balcony of the master bedroom. This style is a local tradition that is found on older houses throughout this area.

The other feature that delights guests is the outdoor shower (see the top photo on p. 71). Equally suited for a summertime cooldown or a rinse after a dip in the river, the outdoor shower exemplifies the link between land and water that Little Elk represents.

Peter Zimmerman, AIA, NCARB, is an architect in Berwyn, PA.

Looking out over the pasture. A cook at work in the kitchen can watch the horses at play in the farm's lower pasture. Photo taken at C on floor plan.

Stretching for the finish line. Showing respect both for the work of the farm and for the craftsmanship of an earlier time, the exposed rafter tails are carved in the shape of horses' heads. Photo taken at G on floor plan.

SOURCES

Michael M. Coldren Company, Inc.
(410) 287-2082
www.coldrencompany.com

A Coastal Remodel Triumphs over Limits

F IVE YEARS AGO, I GOT A CALL FROM DAMIENNE AND VLAD Zeman of Westport, Connecticut. They had bought a starter home a few years earlier and needed design services for a simple renovation of that house. It was on a nice site in Saugatuck Shores, a coastal New England neighborhood of previously unheated vacation shacks slowly being rehabbed into year-round dwellings on postage-stamp-size lots facing saltwater.

Renovation becomes Reinvention

Initially, their needs were relatively modest. They wanted to raise their home to the code-compliant flood level of 13 ft. above mean high tide, to renovate the home's interior, and to redecorate its exterior. The house's plan formed a modified "T" shape; the main section had bedrooms above and living space below, with a simple one-story wing launching off the side containing the kitchen and garage (see the photo above).

A new look amid a regulatory maze. Dormers accent this 12-in-12 pitch roof, which extends over both main wings, creating a saltbox. However, complex local and federal restrictions held the height of the new roof within tight regulatory limits. A nonconforming status as well as budgetary concerns also made it necessary to recycle the two-story portion of the original building (see the photo on the facing page). The footprint is all that remains of the one-story wing. Photos taken at A on floor plan.

A NEW HOUSE MAKES THE BEST OF AN OLD FOOTPRINT

Regulations kept this project from expanding much beyond the original dimensions, so the new plan uses the T–shape of the existing house. The two-story north-south section of the house was recycled with a steeper roof adding a dramatic note to the bedrooms. A master bedroom with a cathedral ceiling tops off the rebuilt east–west section of the house with an upgraded kitchen and garage on the first floor.

SPECS

BEDROOMS: **3**

BATHROOMS: **2½**

SIZE: **2,800 sq. ft.**

COST: **n/a**

COMPLETED: **2000**

LOCATION: **Westport, Connecticut**

ARCHITECT: **Duo Dickinson**

BUILDER: **C & J Construction**

During the design process, the Zemans ultimately decided to address their long-term housing needs. This decision was due partly to their changing needs; they already had one child, and another was on the way by the time construction commenced. The change in plans meant the initial budget grew, and the impact of our expanded design services had to fall within strict local and federal regulations.

Because of our pre-existing, nonconforming status and budgetary concerns, we recycled the two-story portion of the building. The other wing was to be renovated into a more functional kitchen and garage with a new master suite above.

Homeowners Unwind the Red Tape

Virtually every aspect of this home was barely within the building and zoning requirements that would have been imposed on a naked lot. We simply could not have built a new home of this design in this location.

Zoning regulations allowed a small expansion of the existing footprint. Similarly, the height of the building was limited to 26 ft.; the height restriction had to take into account that we were raising the house approximately 3 ft. above its current height to comply with the Coastal Area Management Code.

Custom construction becomes the obvious choice for anyone wanting to build in this context. How do you deal with such extraordinary budgetary and regulatory limits and still create something special? The answer is simple: the investment of time. By investing their own time into working out solutions, homeowners can often solve problems that could be more quickly dealt with by an infusion of raw manpower (and thus dollars).

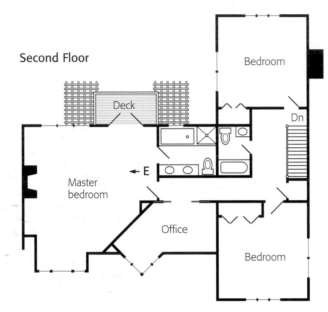

Second Floor

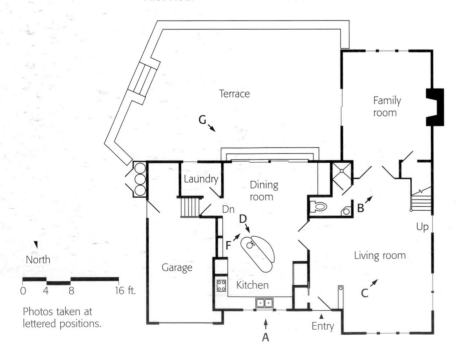

First Floor

North

0 4 8   16 ft.

Photos taken at lettered positions.

Because our firm was working on an hourly basis, our time was tightly monitored. Fortunately, the Zemans took the bull by the horns, tirelessly massaging zoning and building department issues through a maze of hearings, meetings, correspondence, and informal discussions among engineers, surveyors, town officials, the builder, and me. Their aggressive attention to this part of the process allowed us to obtain building permits and approvals in a relatively short time.

Similarly, they assaulted their strident budgetary limitations in a variety of ways. First, they picked C & J Construction of Madison, Connecticut, an out-of-town builder that offered a better price because they were located outside of Fairfield County's aggressive pricing; second, they directly purchased all the custom millwork, many of the lighting fixtures, and much of the hardware. The homeowners also threw themselves into the process of writing checks to suppliers, being responsible for deliveries, and following up on loose ends.

As many homebuilding veterans know, this approach can be a shortcut to errors and finger-pointing. Homeowners' inexperience in construction management often translates into disappointments and recriminations with architects and builders. In this case, though, the Zemans' unstinting attention to detail and seemingly inexhaustible energy ensured that this project would deliver an excellent bang for the buck.

Recycling the Original Plan Pays Off

The homeowners' enthusiasm alone didn't make this project a success. It also required a design that would take advantage of the building's existing plan. Mindful of building and zoning requirements, we had to work almost exclusively within the house's original "T" formation, which conveniently separated the formal front of the house from the informal back, with the service areas to one side on the first floor (see the floor plans on the facing page). The structure is now a 2,800-sq.-ft., three-bedroom, 2½-bath house. The upstairs bedrooms stake out the ends of each wing, with baths nestled between them.

On the rear exterior of the house, the intersecting wings were a natural location for a large-scale terrace off the dining room, which looks over the salt marsh (see the photo below). At the front of the house, the intersection of the wings became the main entry.

Mindful of building and zoning requirements, we had to work almost exclusively within the house's original "T" formation.

Patio doors frame a lovely view. A built-in cabinet serves the dining area. Patio doors provide access to a large terrace overlooking the salt marsh. Photo taken at F on floor plan.

Round and oval windows are placed in key locations. The oval window at the bottom of the stairs adds visual interest, allows natural light to enter, and provides an outside view. Photo taken at C on floor plan.

A cantilevered porch overlooks the marsh. Two large brackets and a large beam support a cantilevered porch off the master bedroom. Trellises with contoured tails flank the porch. Photo taken at G on floor plan.

New Roof Animates the Exterior

The most obvious change in the house is the roof. The roofline swoops just above the entry, which has a curved ceiling. And the 6-in-12 pitch roof gave way to a new 12-in-12 pitch, which extends over the entry and the garage bay, creating a saltbox for the two intersecting wings.

Not so obvious are the laminated beams used to pick up some of the point loads generated at the intersections of roofs. The new 12-in-12 pitch roofs needed only engineered collar ties along with prefabricated steel hurricane ties installed at all rafter/plate connections to provide stiffness.

The gable dormer over the garage provides visual interest as well as additional headroom in the master bedroom; another smaller dormer projects at a 45-degree angle with a multifaceted roof just above the entrance. To distinguish these dormers further, the head casings of the individual win-

dows in the gabled dormers rise as the gable roof ascends; the sills on the angled dormer windows fall as they progress down the main roof. To make the dormers more a part of the roof, they were sided with tongue-and-groove red-cedar siding, in contrast with the surrounding house, which is finished in white-cedar shingles.

The same head/sill interplay evident in the dormers is echoed in the heads of the kitchen windows below. In addition, a curved transom window with splayed sides above the entry door complements the swoop in the roof (see the photo on p. 77). Round and oval windows are set at key points on the exterior: at gable peaks, at the bottom of the stairs (see the photo on the facing page) and in bathrooms.

In addition, the muntin patterns on many windows follow a cruciform motif, with the vertical and horizontal bars creating square panes at the top and elongated panes below. The round and oval windows are similar, but rather than the cruciform, they have a simple crosshairs pattern.

We added several other elements on the exterior to enrich the overall form. At the entry roof overhang, a large knee brace was added. In the rear, the tails of the cantilevered framing that support the trellis/porch off the master bedroom were carefully sculpted (see the photo above) and supported by an octagonal beam and a pair of knee braces.

The tapered chimney uses both trim and a flared, lead-coated copper cap to add distinction to this focal point. The eaves of the house are rendered to complement and unify the rest of the exterior trim details as well as the roof forms.

Round and oval windows are set at key points on the exterior: at gable peaks, at the bottom of the stairs, and in bathrooms.

Curved-top armoire complements the angled ceiling. This stylish built-in closet neatly tucks into the voids alongside the fireplace in the master bedroom. Photo taken at E on floor plan.

Durable and cost-effective materials throughout. Painted drywall, hardwood floors, and solid-wood trim combine successfully to create a modest yet elegant interior, as in this family-room sitting area. Photo taken at B on floor plan.

FACING PAGE The island defines the kitchen area. With its curved front wrapped in cherry wainscot, the island serves as a divider between the kitchen and dining room. The bar top is teak, and the countertops are granite. Photo taken at D on floor plan.

SOURCES

C & J Construction
Madison, Connecticut
(203) 740-0532

Modest Choices Elsewhere Permit an Elegant Kitchen

The kitchen, whose details the owners took on with gusto, became the heart of an open floor plan (see the photo on the facing page). Cherry frame-and-panel cabinetry was used throughout, including the front panels of the refrigerator and dishwasher, making them less conspicuous.

The island is set at an angle for easier access. The curved front is wrapped in cherry wainscot, the bar top is oiled teak, and the countertops are granite.

We integrated the kitchen cabinets into the window trim over the kitchen sink. Two cabinets with glass-panel doors fill the niche created by the smaller windows, which flank the larger window over the kitchen sink.

In addition to the kitchen, the interior finishes of hardwood flooring and solid-wood trim used in the den and throughout the house are durable and simple (see the photo at right above). Painted drywall became dramatic in the master-bedroom suite after we fleshed out the shapes resulting from the intersecting rooflines (see the photo at left above).

Duo Dickinson is an architect in Madison, CT. He is the author of the forthcoming book, *The House You Build* (The Taunton Press, Inc., 2004).

Detailing Decks
over Living Space

The second-floor and third-floor decks were the problem. With a footprint limited by wetlands, this house on the Florida coast rose up, not out. Consequently, two decks at the central tower, or crow's nest, had to be built above finished interior spaces.

CHARLIE AND SALLY WILLIAMSON'S LOT ON APALACHICOLA Bay looked plenty big until I saw the wetlands survey. I realized then that we would have to build up instead of out. But a multi-story house meant two decks built over finished interior space, an architectural bugaboo I always avoid. However, Charlie is a construction waterproofing consultant. We discussed the situation over a few beers and decided to damn the torpedoes and go full speed ahead.

TORCH-DOWN ROOFING WATERPROOFS THE DECK.

The 3-ply welded roofing (base sheet, interply, and cap sheet) combined with self-adhering bituminous membrane used as flashing keeps out the water. A two-layer foundation drainage mat goes over this roofing. The top layer is filter fabric that keeps debris that could block the flow of water off the roof. The second layer is a rigid plastic mesh that provides a clear drainage path and a cushion that protects the roofing from the sleepers above. Underlying all of this is a ¾-in. plywood roof deck sloped a minimum of ⅛ in. per ft.

Crow's nest

Second-floor deck

Removable pressure-treated 2x6 decking on pressure-treated 2x4 sleepers

Drainage mat

Cap sheet

Interply

Base sheet

Self-adhering bituminous-membrane flashing

¾-in. plywood deck slopes at minimum ⅛ in. per ft.

Pitch the Roof So That it Drains

The best roofing materials can still leak when they're applied to a deck that holds water, or ponds. So good waterproofing begins by sloping the deck at least ⅛ in. per ft. to drain the water; ¼ in. per ft. is even better. On Charlie's house, the carpenters sistered 2x6s to some floor joists and tapered others to get the slope. We sheathed the decks with ¾-in. plywood to be sure the deck sheathing wouldn't sag and make ponds.

The second-floor deck simply drains onto the roof below. But the crow's nest deck is enclosed by kneewalls, and the roof over the deck below actually comes above the crow's nest floor. We pitched the deck toward this roof and raised the bottom plate of the kneewall, forming a scupper to drain the water. It drains under the kneewall into a gutter that has been mounted beneath the roof overhang below.

A Foundation Drainage Mat Provides Extra Protection

The roofing that Charlie recommended is a 3-ply, heat-weld system from Johns Manville (see sources at right) installed over the plywood decking. All the exterior walls that intersect decks are wrapped with Polyguard 650 (see sources), a self-adhering bituminous membrane consisting of a high-strength polyethylene backing laminated to a thick (60-mil) layer of rubberized asphalt. We brought the Polyguard about 6 in. onto the base sheet of the roofing to serve as flashing and went over the Polyguard flange with the remaining two layers of roofing.

Next, we installed a layer of J-Drain 1000 (see sources), a ¼-in.-thick sheet of crush-proof plastic mesh core wrapped in filter fabric. The J-Drain is laid loose on top of the roofing. Normally used as a drainage mat around foundations, in this case the J-Drain provides a layer of padding that protects the underlying waterproofing membrane, and it lets water drain under the sleepers that are supporting the deck.

Two-by-six decking screwed to pressure-treated 2x4 sleepers forms the walking surface. The sleepers run parallel to the slope of the deck to allow drainage.

This composite of materials provides a waterproof membrane that will flex and not crack as the wood framing deflects under load. Should leaks occur, the deck and J-Drain can be lifted and the roof inspected and repaired (see the drawing on the facing page).

Charlie and Sally's house survived Hurricane Opal during construction and then two no-name storms that have passed by since. Opal devastated the nearby Apalachicola Marina, and the lot flooded during all three storms. But the roof didn't leak.

John Phelps is an architect and wooden boat builder with Phelps Browning Sullivan Architects Inc. in Atlanta, GA.

This composite of materials provides a waterproof membrane that will flex and not crack as the wood framing deflects under load.

SOURCES

Johns Manville
800-654-3103
www.jm.com

Polyguard Products Inc.
800-541-4994
www.polyguardproducts.com

JDR Enterprises Inc.
Alphretta, GA 30043
800-843-7569

The Bridge House

MY CLIENTS FIRST SAW THE SITE FOR THEIR NEW HOUSE from a boat. The land, called Sally's Rocks, is on the shore of Narragansett Bay in Jamestown, Rhode Island, across the strait from Newport, Rhode Island. Sally's Rocks has commanding views of the water and lies just south of the Newport Bridge, on Conanicut Island.

Like most sailors, my clients would rather be aboard a ship than ashore; they would rather be varnishing their boat than cutting grass. Also like most sailors, they appreciate fine woodwork and good, solid construction, and they are intrigued by new materials and systems. In fact, the Bridge House, as it became known, was designed and built by sailors. Lest the house-as-boat metaphor appear too simple, we kept in mind during each phase of design and construction that—like a fine yacht—the house had to withstand island winds and willful weather. And to accommodate the family's seagoing life, the house had to rival a yacht in efficiency.

Sheds, gables and a gambrel. Bound into a cohesive whole by its shingle cladding, this new shingle-style house unites a variety of seemingly unrelated roofs into a pleasing, asymmetrical composition. Photo taken at A on floor plan.

Organized Around a Central Hall

Like the passageway down the center of a ship, the hallway in the Bridge House leads to all of the rooms on the first floor. The hall is widest near the entry, where the formal stair engages the foyer. The public rooms are distinct and separate from one another, but they are linked by wide passageways.

Floor-plan key

1 Living room
2 Den
3 Kitchen
4 Dining room
5 Study
6 Front hall
7 Back hall
8 Garage
9 Bedroom
10 Guest bedroom

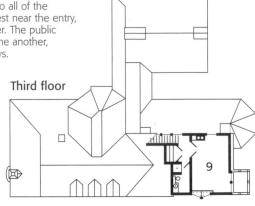

Third floor

SPECS

BEDROOMS: **5**

BATHROOMS: **5**

HEATING SYSTEM: **Three-zone, oil-fired forced air**

SIZE: **3,800 sq. ft.**

COST: **N/A**

COMPLETED: **1993**

LOCATION: **Jamestown, Rhode Island**

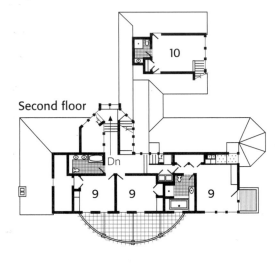

Second floor

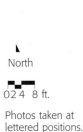

North

0 2 4 8 ft.

Photos taken at lettered positions.

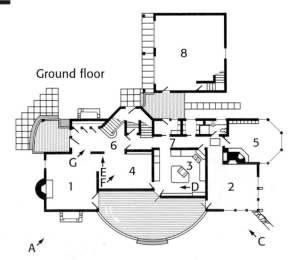

Ground floor

The Shingle Style Is Alive and Well

Toward the end of the 19th century, New England architects and legions of talented builders forged a new residential style that took its name from the cedar shingles used to cover both roofs and sidewalls. Shingle-style houses drew their inspiration from, among other influences, the fanciful shapes of Queen Anne Victorian houses and the sturdy, rooted-to-the-ground earthiness of Richardsonian Romanesque buildings. Because they were primarily vacation houses, shingle-style homes were festooned with decks, porches, eyebrow dormers and damsel-in-the-tower bump-outs wherever they seemed appropriate.

Today, shingle-style houses are more popular than ever along Rhode Island's shoreline. They have become the vernacular, and to keep within that vernacular, my clients wanted a shingle-style house large enough for themselves and their three children. They entertain frequently, so we needed to provide informal and formal spaces that revolved around the kitchen. The rooms had to be separate and distinct from one another, while nevertheless linked.

We decided early on to use a stressed-skin panel system (more on that to follow). The system required careful integration and coordination of the structural and operational systems: plumbing, heating, mechanical and electrical. There couldn't be a slapdash layering of systems.

A Central Hall Links the Rooms

A shingle-style house typically uses a central hall as the organizing element, with most of the rooms radiating from the hall. Some shingle-style houses are deep or boxy, making it difficult for light to penetrate to the center of the house. We decided to stretch this house into a linear form to catch the light better (see the floor plans on the facing page).

Inside, a long, telescoping passageway becomes the spine for the house, like a ship's passageway. At one end lies the public entrance hall and stairway (see the top photo at right), with generous openings to the living and dining rooms.

At the core of the house, the kitchen is the crossroads between the public and private sides of the house, as well as being adjacent to the deck. Across the hall from the kitchen, the mudroom leads to the garage, the breezeway and the rear yard. The hallway narrows as it leads to the den and ultimately to the study, which forms the bow of the house with a hexagonal bay. I like to think of the study as the "navigational station": Tucked away and private, it is the place where the owners chart their course.

The bowed deck, reached through the kitchen and the living room, links the public and private portions of the house (see the bottom photo at right). A trellis shades the redwood deck without making it dark, as a covered porch might. The deck reads as a ship's deck, a place to catch ocean breezes and watch the activity in Newport Harbor.

A stairway fit for an entrance. Engaging the entry vestibule at an angle, the primary stairway ascends into a light-filled bay that projects from the otherwise straight north wall. Photo taken at G on floor plan.

On the south side of the house, the bowed deck juts out to catch the sun and the breeze off the bay. A portion of the deck is notched into the shingle-style house, which works to link the interior rooms with one another. In the distance, the Newport Bridge spans Narragansett Bay. Photo taken at B on floor plan.

Big brackets support a small deck. On the second floor, a deck off the master bedroom overlooks the children's fenced-in yard. To the far right, the bumped-up gables in the garage allow taller windows in the guest room. Photo taken at C on floor plan.

Glued-together panels make walls and roof. Under the shingles, panels of expanded polystyrene foam and OSB make up the structure and insulate the house. The result is a tight building envelope that helps reduce heating costs. During the frigid winter of 1993-94, heating bills totaled less than $900. Photo taken at C on floor plan.

Roof Forms
Change as Necessary

The 20-ft.-wide core of the house moves from a gable end over the entry to a gambrel end over the bedrooms at the east end of the house. On the second floor, a small deck off the master bedroom is supported by a pair of massive brackets (see the photo on the facing page).

The 20-ft.-wide core of the house is flanked by an 11-ft.-wide shed that shelters the secondary spaces, such as the mudroom, the laundry and the bathroom along the north side of the house. The shed is interrupted by the hipped, hexagonal mass of the roof over the stairway, then emerges again to wrap around the southern end of the house, where it shelters the entry. Part of the fun of the shingle-style house is the flexibility given the designer. Do you need a space? Graft it onto or carve it out of the

shingled mass. In the Bridge House, both the entry and the deck on the east side of the house are carved into the building. Typical of shingle style, the house has a romantic asymmetry of parts within a balanced composition.

Stressed-Skin-Panel System

Builder Doug Shear, owner of Newport Housewrights, first suggested using the stressed-skin panel system, in which the building is composed of thick (6½ in. to 8½ in.) slabs of expanded-polystyrene foam insulation sandwiched between oriented-strand-board (OSB) panels (see the photo above). This system is the land-bound cousin of the sophisticated carbon-fiber-and-foam sandwich construction currently used on racing boats.

We used wooden I-joists to free-span the 20-ft.-wide core of the house. Standard stud

Frame-and-panel trim.
Honduran-mahogany trim emphasizes the yachtlike soul of the Bridge House. The sapele panels are veneer over a birch-plywood substrate. Photo taken at E on floor plan.

As in a well-designed boat, there is no clear dividing line in the finished house between the carpentry and the cabinetwork.

Built-in cabinetry in the formal dining room. The Bridge House has distinct rooms instead of an open floor plan. The dining room's formality is emphasized by the finely wrought cabinetwork for dishware and table linens. Photo taken at F on floor plan.

walls bear on the I-joists for our nonstructural partitions. Both plumbing and electrical systems are in these interior walls. Electrical outlets in the exterior walls are located in channels that were cut with a router on site.

As the panels go up, their joints are filled with urethane foam, which glues the panels together and seals against air leaks. The windows and the doors are also foamed in place. The result is a well-insulated, super-strong house that has great lateral resistance to wind loads. So far, it has withstood gusty 60-knot northeasters without a shudder.

Seven Coats of Varnish

As in a well-designed boat, there is no clear dividing line in the finished house between the carpentry and the cabinetwork. The Housewrights' crew, along with woodworker Joseph Yoffa, constructed and assembled on

A wide kitchen ties the dining room to the family room. Many paths lead through the kitchen, but foot traffic doesn't encroach on the cook because the primary food-preparation areas are next to the island cooktop and the sink. Photo taken at D on floor plan.

site the intricate stair railing and the frame-and-panel mahogany and sapele (see the photo at left on the facing page). In the dining room, they extended the mahogany detailing with built-in china cupboards (see the photo at right on the facing page). The kitchen, on the other hand, is less formal. It has painted cabinets and sandy-colored plastic-laminate surfaces on the counters and the island top (see the photo above).

The owners have lived one year in their new house and report that it performs equally well in winter storms and summer hot spells. The house could probably roll 30° without a thing falling out of place. It's tight, strong, and livable, with no leaks to date.

James Estes is an architect working in Newport, RI. His firm, Estes/Twombly has received over 90 design awards and has been published in numerous books and magazines.

Rebirth of a California Beach House

BEFORE I MET THEM, MARK AND KATHLEEN SULLIVAN HAD
spent 30 summers in their tiny cottage a few blocks from
California's Monterey Bay. The house, which is in the town of
Capitola, was filled with memories—and terminally bad structural detailing.
Sagging like an old saddle, the roof sheltered a floor as wavy as the nearby
surf. The house bore witness to many years of wear and tear from an active
family of five.

Now, with their kids grown and retirement drawing near, the Sullivans
were looking to rebuild and enlarge the cottage (see the photo above) and
turn it into their primary residence.

Landlocked cottage. Surrounded by streets on three sides and a public access on the fourth, this house is sitting on a zoning island. The architect borrowed vernacular shapes and details from other houses in the area to maintain the bay-side bungalow spirit. Photo taken at B on floor plan.

A nautical touch. Nicknamed the crow's nest, this round, cantilevered deck adds a little salty flavor to the exterior. The horizontal lines of the deck help unify the shapes and angles of the tower and the sleeping porch. Photo taken at A on floor plan.

Strict Local Ordinances Limit the Design

California beach-town lots are typically small, and the houses that sprung up on them during the first half of the century were inexpensive, informal bungalows. Although the neighborhoods grew up with little planning, the casual, unself-conscious results are worth protecting from over-development. To that end, the local design committee wisely limits lot coverage and building height.

The Sullivans' lot is small, even by beach-town standards. It's a 50-ft. square island surrounded by roads on three sides and a sidewalk on the fourth. Local codes allow the square footage of the house, plus the garage, to be no more than 65% of the lot and a maximum height of 27 ft. In addition, the town requires 10-ft. side-yard setbacks and a 20-ft. front-yard setback. This requirement was a problem. Applying contemporary setbacks would have meant reducing the footprint of the house, includ-

ing garage, to a mere 20 ft. by 30 ft. Fortunately, the planning department chose to let us maintain the footprint of the original house. Its garage was directly on the northeast property line, so staying within the existing footprint worked to our advantage. The design-committee members agreed to this exception after they saw our preliminary plans for the house. They were pleased that the new house maintained the spirit of the neighborhood. As a result, the committee members did what they could to make it happen.

Familiar Materials, Shapes and a Tower of Light

To maintain the neighborhood's spirit, I studied the forms and materials of the nearby houses. There were plenty of unifying themes: shingle or board-and-batten wood siding, multi-pane windows, rounded rafter tails, exposed roof decking along the eaves, hip roofs and a tendency to break up the form of the house into a collection of con-

A Tight Fit
Squeezed into an existing footprint, this bungalow near Monterey Bay was rebuilt and expanded into two floors in order to become a primary residence.

SPECS

BEDROOMS: 2
(including sleeping porch)
BATHROOMS: 2
HEATING SYSTEM:
Forced Hot Air (gas)
SIZE: 1,625 sq. ft.
COST: $142.00 per sq. ft.
COMPLETED: 1994
LOCATION: Capitola, California

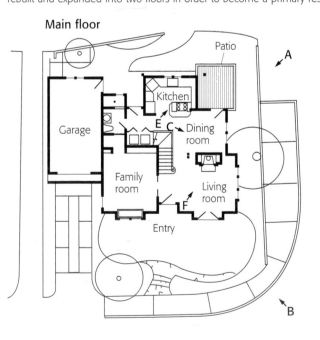

Main floor

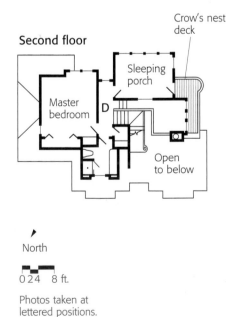

Second floor

North

0 2 4   8 ft.

Photos taken at lettered positions.

nected volumes. I worked all of these characteristics into the exterior, along with a tower that nears the 27-ft. height limit.

Towers are common to other nearby homes that have views of the water. The Sullivans don't have such a view, so this tower serves another purpose. Topped with a hip roof and ringed with windows, this tower is designed to let light deep inside the house. A deck adjacent to the tower adds a horizontal plane that helps bring down the scale of the tower. The circular bump-out projecting from the corner of the deck was christened the crow's nest (see the photo on p. 97).

The Sleeping Porch Moves Up

A favorite room in the old house was the sleeping porch, and the Sullivans wanted to make sure the new house carried on the tradition. To expand the main floor, I moved the new sleeping porch and the master bedroom to the upper floor (see the floor plan on the facing page).

On the main floor, a dramatic freestanding fireplace (see the photo below) pulls attention to the cathedral ceiling over the living room and separates the living room from the dining space below the tower.

Jam-packed but wide open. Almost the entire house is visible from the main entry. The board-and-batten siding above the fireplace accents the vertical elements of the interior, and shuttered doors above the railing open into the sleeping porch. Photo taken at F on floor plan.

The compact kitchen has more appliance storage and work areas than many kitchens twice its size.

It may not allow for views, but the tower provides the overhead light for this cozy dining area. Photo taken at D on floor plan.

Unlike most ceilings, the one over the dining table lets light, which comes from the tower, filter to the first floor (see the photo above). The ceiling—also the floor of the tower room—is ¾-in.-thick Lexan, a polycarbonate sheet material tough enough to stop a bullet.

The Lexan is carried by whitewashed Douglas-fir beams on 10-in. centers. Our builders, Tom Howland and Patrick

Echelbarger, affixed the Lexan to the beams with screws driven into oversize holes in the plastic sheeting. Like other plastic sheet goods, Lexan expands and contracts a lot. The oversize holes allow the Lexan to move a little without cracking. The flooring is sandblasted in stripes to suggest the appearance of decking(see the bottom photo on the facing page). We put the sandblasted

A compact but comfortable kitchen. Smart layout lets this kitchen feature multiple work centers and every major appliance within its tiny confines. The spaces on both sides of the wall-oven cabinetry are appliance garages. Photo taken at E on floor plan.

Translucent decking lets in the light. Clear Lexan was sandblasted to give the appearance of decking. Photo taken at C on floor plan.

surface up to give the floor a little bit of traction.

Storage Space at a Premium

For the Sullivans, moving from a much larger house into this cottage made storage space a priority, and we tried to make use of every accessible area. We squeezed a washer-and-dryer closet under the stairs and a cold-storage pantry beneath the stair landing. This pantry is only about 4 ft. tall (to get to the back, you've got to crawl), but it's cooled by an underfloor air inlet, and the pantry has a solid door with a full thermal seal to hold in the cool air.

The compact kitchen has more appliance storage and work areas than many kitchens twice its size (see the photo on the facing page). The peninsula countertop has an eating bar on one side with a down-vented cooktop on the other. We even turned the wedge-shaped dead spaces on both sides of the oven cabinet into appliance garages. When the weather is pleasant, the pass-through window above the counter allows the Sullivans to use their patio for outdoor dining.

Tobin T. Dougherty is an architect with offices in Palo Alto, CA, and Sun Valley, ID.

Home on the Beach

SOMETIMES A LINGERING IMAGE IS SO POWERFUL THAT IT can change your life. Traveling through Greece in 1974, Beth Kaminstein and Ron Levy took a side trip to an island in the Aegean. Ron and Beth are both potters, and in their travels they make a point of visiting other ceramic artists. On the island they met a potter named George, who had a studio on the beach. After loading his kiln, George would take a swim in the warm, clear water and fish for his dinner while the pots fired in the kiln.

This image of a balance between work, play and nature stayed with Ron and Beth. Fifteen years later, they decided to leave their long-time home in New York City and start a new life on a Florida beach. They found their spot in Islamorada, on Upper Matecumbe Key. There they bought a long, narrow waterfront lot that included a 720-sq.-ft. house made out of cast-in-place concrete (see the photo above). Built to be hurricane proof, it was one of 26 houses constructed in 1936 after a hurricane devastated the island. The Red Cross donated the raw materials, and the Federal Relief Administration provided the labor to rebuild the homes of families that survived the storm.

Circulation tower. A bridge reached by a three-story tower connects the old house, in the background, with the new studio on the right. Screens made of galvanized hat channel and expanded metal lath envelope the bridge and the studio and will one day be covered with vines (above). The notch in the tower is on the observation deck. Photo taken at A on floor plan.
Open to the sea breezes. The stair tower stands behind the original cottage, which has been outfitted with a new deck and awnings (facing page). Photo taken at B on floor plan.

The new pottery studio is below the sleeping quarters, which puts the living spaces above the high-tide code requirement and the studio at truck level. Photo taken at C on floor plan.

. . . the roof detailing is designed to keep direct heat gain to a minimum, beginning with the reflective surface of the Galvalume metal roofing.

Over the years the house never fell victim to the high winds and the surging tides of a hurricane. Instead, the corrosive, salty environment was destroying the house at a more tortoiselike pace. Swollen by rust, the rebar had popped portions of concrete off the walls and the roof.

Ron and Beth wanted to preserve the historic structure, solid relic that it was, before it got any worse. They also needed to add a studio for their pottery business, and that's how I got involved. Ron and Beth learned about the Jersey Devil Design/Build partnership when they read about our Space-Age Cracker House. They liked the way that house is arranged with its bedrooms over a large workspace, and they appreciated its passive-cooling strategies and the metal detailing. Soon the couple hired Jersey Devil to create a compound of buildings that met their needs. Our master plan called for renovating the original house and transforming it into the kitchen and the public rooms.

We'd then build a separate structure for the studio and the bedrooms and provide guest quarters on top of the existing carport.

Linked by the Tower

Several code-imposed conditions exerted themselves before we put any ideas on paper. Because the waterfront is densely populated, the local building department is worried about people building more than one house on small ocean-front lots. So new structures on the site had to be connected to the original house. Also, living quarters now must be elevated at least 5 ft. above mean tide. No problem. That stipulation meshed perfectly with our original intentions, and we went ahead to propose a new two-story structure with a pottery studio below a bedroom wing (see the photo above).

In a harsh climate, covered paths wouldn't be a practical way to link the detached elements of this house. In south Florida, how-

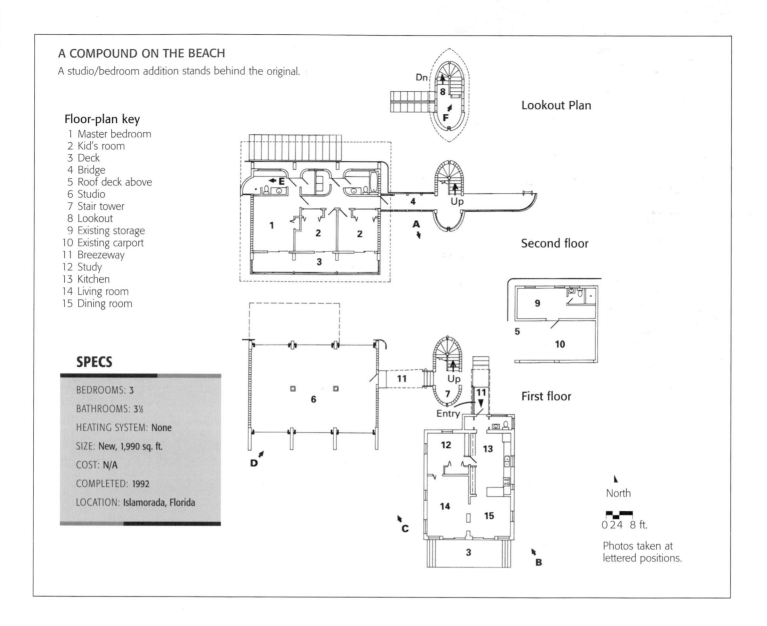

A COMPOUND ON THE BEACH

A studio/bedroom addition stands behind the original.

Lookout Plan

Floor-plan key

1 Master bedroom
2 Kid's room
3 Deck
4 Bridge
5 Roof deck above
6 Studio
7 Stair tower
8 Lookout
9 Existing storage
10 Existing carport
11 Breezeway
12 Study
13 Kitchen
14 Living room
15 Dining room

Second floor

First floor

SPECS

BEDROOMS: **3**

BATHROOMS: **3½**

HEATING SYSTEM: **None**

SIZE: **New, 1,990 sq. ft.**

COST: **N/A**

COMPLETED: **1992**

LOCATION: **Islamorada, Florida**

North

0 2 4 8 ft.

Photos taken at lettered positions.

ever, the mild temperatures invite outdoor living. To satisfy the linkage portion of the code requirements, we connected the original house, its carport and the new studio with a combination of breezeways and bridges (see the floor plan above).

All paths lead through a centrally located three-story stair tower (see the photo on p. 103). The tower eliminates the need for a stair in the studio/bedroom wing, but more importantly, it provides a dramatic architectural focal point for the compound. At the tower's second-floor landing, a covered bridge leads to the bedroom wing over the pottery studio. In the other direction, an

open walkway runs to the patio atop the carport roof. The tower's third floor is an observation deck.

The stair-tower roof is supported in part by two see-through columns that look like giant bicycle chains, bisecting the tower vertically. The columns are composed of a pair of 2x12s, separated by 6-in. sections of aluminum irrigation pipe (see the photo at right on p. 106). The spaces between the tube sections admit ocean breezes and daylight into the tower and create a delicate pattern of reflected artificial light at night. Beth picked the bright fuchsia color for the columns and the beam they support, and as

Our master plan called for renovating the original house and transforming it into the kitchen and the public rooms.

Metal soffits. Marine-green corrugated steel comes inside the house to cover the soffits, such as this detail in the master bathroom. Thin birch plywood covers the arcing ceiling. Photo taken at E on floor plan.

Lipstick columns. Painted fuchsia, built-up columns made of 2x12s carry the ridge beam of the tower roof. The silver spacers between the 2x12s are 6-in. sections of aluminum irrigation pipe. Photo taken at F on floor plan.

soon as the columns were painted, they were christened the "lipstick columns."

To withstand a serious hurricane, the first two floors of the tower had to be reinforced cast concrete. For the sake of economy, we built the third floor with studs and plywood. Then we clad the tower with a metal skin to give its exterior a unified pattern. We chose corrugated Galvalume to emphasize the tower's vertical nature (see sources on the facing page).

Low-Maintenance Finishes

Ron and Beth want to spend their time living and working in the house—not fixing it. Consequently, we used materials that will last—even next to the ocean. The exterior fasteners used for the structure are stainless steel. The 5-V crimp metal roof and corrugated siding are warranted for 20 years. We

also used corrugated Galvalume, prepainted marine green, for indoor and outdoor soffits (see the photo at right above).

Concrete is another low-maintenance material. But because it's porous, concrete should be treated—when used near the ocean—to minimize the chances that salt water will seep into the concrete and corrode the rebar. To that end, Ron coated all exterior vertical surfaces of the concrete with Chemstop, from Tamms Industries, a clear sealer for concrete that isn't exposed to traffic. Ron used another product by Tamms, Siloxane, to seal floors and passageways (see sources).

Passive Cooling

Florida is famous for its balmy winters and its hot, muggy summers. Most people resort to air conditioning to make a house bearable when it gets hot, but Ron and Beth wanted to take a more passive approach to keeping their house comfortable. Here's how we did it.

To take advantage of the prevailing breeze off the ocean, both the leeward and windward sides of the bedroom wing have operable windows to allow unrestricted airflow. The windows are the awning type (hinged at the top, the bottom swings up and away from the house), which can be left open, even when it rains. All partition walls (except the bathroom and the master bedroom) stop shy of the ceiling for air circulation. To keep clothes from getting musty, the closets have louvered doors and ventilation grills in their back walls. The breeze is pretty reliable, but if it fails, the four ceiling fans can stir up the air.

The 7½-in.-thick concrete ceiling of the studio is also the finished floor of the bedroom wing. This massive hunk of concrete, along with the cast-concrete pillars that support it and the roof, also helps to keep the air cool (see the photo at right). Generous roof overhangs limit the sun's exposure on the concrete.

Finally, the roof detailing is designed to keep direct heat gain to a minimum, beginning with the reflective surface of the Galvalume metal roofing. About 95% of the radiant heat that gets past the roof skin is stopped by the radiant barrier above the R-19 fiberglass insulation. As the heat builds up above the radiant barrier, the convection loop between the continuous soffit and ridge vents gets rid of it. We went ahead and installed air conditioning ducts in the bedroom wing (for resale value) but no air-conditioning unit has ever been purchased. It doesn't get hot enough inside to need one.

The Living Screen

This diverse group of buildings needed an architectural device to tie them together on the street side. We did that with a screen of galvanized metal that begins at the carport, continues across the tower bridge and around the side of the studio that faces the

At the wheel. Concrete pillars flank matching roll-up garage doors on opposite sides of the pottery studio. The doors can be retracted to let sea breezes circulate cool air throughout the building. Photo taken at D on floor plan.

road. Jersey Devil partner Jim Adamson built the screen out of galvanized hat channel, which is typically used as purlins in metal buildings. The hat channel is affixed in a grid to the sides of the buildings. High-profile galvanized expanded metal lath (typically used for reinforcing plaster) is the gauzy fabric that covers the grid.

The screen serves as an armature for tropical vines that will shade the house and buffer highway noise and vehicular vapors. The passion-fruit has taken root first. One day it will wrap a leafy cape around the building, full of flowers and oxygen that will help the complex breathe.

Steve Badanes is a partner in the peripatetic design/build collaborative Jersey Devil (www.jersey-devildesignbuild.com).

SOURCES

For Galvalume
MBCI
281-445-8555
www.mbci.com

For Chemstop and Siloxane
Tamms Industries
800-862-2667
www.tamms.com

Classical Details
in a Harsh Environment

THE FIRST TIME I VISITED THE BUILDING SITE, I WAS
humbled by Mother Nature. With my head bowed, and a site
plan held tightly to my chest, I made my way against 45-mph
onshore winds and walked to the eastern-most edge of the property. When
I looked up, squinting against the blowing sand, I was standing on the lip
of a sand dune, about 80 ft. above the Atlantic Ocean. Even during the tail
end of a Nor'easter, it was easy to see why the site had been selected as a
place to build a house.

The views were breathtaking. The ferocity of the weather added to the
drama of the site. This section of New England coastline is frequently buf-
feted by gales, and over the last decade, the beaches have taken the brunt
of three hurricanes. In short, this was a location that would test the integrity of any building.

Craftsmen built this coastal
house to withstand hurricane
winds, meticulous architects,
and exacting clients who put quality
above all else.

The construction took almost two years and incorporated the skills of dozens of tradesmen, including 14 carpenters.

The people who owned the property wanted a house that would stand up to the weather while looking as if it had occupied the site for decades. They sought a style that would complement the land and reflect the most beautiful aspects of the area's traditional architecture.

Having built houses for more than two decades, I have become a firm believer in the absolute importance of beginning a project with a complete set of plans. Good plans are not those found in plan books or in the back pages of home magazines.

The architect of the house, Allan Greenberg of Greenwich, Connecticut, is known for his adherence to the classical tradition. Given his reputation for strict attention to detail and the client's demand for a beautifully crafted building, it should have come as no surprise to me when, prior to the commencement of the project, I received a 160-page project manual. A brief review of this volume, and I quickly learned that perfection would be the only acceptable standard. This was a job where cost took a position secondary to the quality of the work. The construction took almost two years and incorporated the skills of dozens of tradesmen, including 14 carpenters. A field architect from Greenberg's office reviewed the project's progress at least once a week. There were also two site inspections from representatives of the structural engineering firm.

Engineered to Withstand 135-mph Winds

Because the house occupies a site that would constantly test its structural integrity, it was engineered to withstand 135-mph winds. The specifications required many components not regularly incorporated in a house in this part of the country: glue-laminated beams, hurricane ties and hold-downs (see the photo below), special concrete requirements—including slump tests for all the transit mix delivered to the job—even the framing lumber was unusual.

For a building to withstand 135-mph winds, a strong frame must be connected to a strong, well-engineered foundation. In this case the foundation, starting with the 1-ft. thick footings, which ranged in width from 1 ft. up to 6 ft., depending on their location and function, was reinforced with both vertical and horizontal rebar.

The concrete specs came from the engineer and, like any good recipe, all ingredients were provided to our ready-mix company well before the project began. The mix specified a 3,000-psi ¾-in. pumpable product with the proportions of cement, fine aggregate, coarse aggregate, water content, water-reducing agent, air-entraining agent and the instruction that the batch weights were not to be field adjusted for moisture content, all spelled out in a series of construction memos.

In addition to the rebar and standard anchor bolts, at numerous critical points 1-in. threaded rods were placed in the concrete to provide connection points for hold-downs that would secure the framing from uplift. In many locations dozens of hold-downs for a variety of wood-to-concrete connections augmented the normal anchor bolts.

We used #1 dense-grade southern yellow pine for the framing. This wood is relatively knot-free, very strong, hard and incredibly

Hurricane straps. Typical of the detailing throughout the house, every rafter was fastened to the walls with galvanized metal straps.

Shear wall. One of two shear walls in the house, this gable end was strengthened with 6x6 timbers that run from the foundation to the rafters. The wall was sheathed on both sides with ¾-in. plywood.

heavy. There were a lot of aching arms at the end of this framing job. Except where pressure-treated southern yellow pine products were called for, kiln-dried southern yellow pine was used throughout the frame.

Shear Walls

To minimize racking or lateral motion during storms, the house frame was designed with shear walls at two locations: one at a gable end (see the photo above) and one centrally located in the interior of the house.

The integrity of the shear walls depends on the careful adherence to their design. From the concrete, 1-in. threaded rods were connected to Simpson hold-downs bolted with ⅝-in.-dia. bolts to the 6x6 posts that augmented the 2x6 wall framing. The shear walls were sheathed on both sides with ¾-in. CDX plywood that was glued with construction adhesive and nailed off every 8 in. Where the roof sheathing meets the top plate of the shear wall, the sheathing is glued and then nailed with two rows of 10d nails 6 in. o. c.

The studs in the shear walls were tied to the plates with steel stud-plate ties. At the top of the walls, the rafters were held to the plates with steel hurricane anchors. The tops of all the rafters were held to the ridge with sloped or sloped-and-skewed hangers as the location required.

The fasteners used throughout the house were chosen for their holding capacity, corrosion resistance and shear strength. All Simpson Strong-Tie connectors were held in place with nails made by Simpson specifically to meet the load design of these connectors. If we had used regular framing nails or any other fasteners, it would have compromised the function of the various ties and connectors. The framing nails were fullhead, either stainless steel or mechanically galvanized. During one framing inspection I told the engineer that if the Simpson Company could fabricate an eyebolt big enough, the whole house could be picked up in one piece.

Keeping Out the Water

Because water is the main culprit in the decay of wood-frame construction, we tried to keep water away from wood. Where that was not possible, our efforts went toward channeling off the water. Where metal flashing was called for, we used 20-oz. lead-coated copper. Lighter-weight 16-oz. copper is commonly used in residential

Tight to the weather. Utmost care was taken to waterproof the house. The soldered 20-oz. lead-coated copper is typical of the house's flashing details. All doors and windows had soldered head flashings. A soldered flashing also protects the bottoms of doors, windows and gable vents.

construction. Many of the flashing details called for the use of both the lead-coated copper and a self-sealing bituminous membrane called Ice & Water Shield, made by W. R. Grace Construction Products (see sources on p. 116).

A soldered head flashing was used over exterior doors, windows and gable vents. A 20-oz. lead-coated copper pan was soldered in place for all the door openings. A soldered flashing also protects the bottoms of windows and gable vents (see the photo above).

The two semicircular bays on the ocean side of the house were a metal smith's nightmare. Paul J. Cazeault & Sons of Orleans, Massachusetts, did the flashing work. The master-bedroom exterior wall incorporates a door and six banked, tilt-turn windows. The flashing of the six windows serves as a counterflashing to the wall flashing below, so it had to incorporate the pan flashing for the door. Small cuts were made in the flashing so that it could be bent to conform to the 9-ft. 1-in. radius of the bay. After the desired shape was attained, the cuts were soldered to make an impermeable metal membrane.

The house's roofs—hips, valleys, ridges and eaves—have weatherproofing components of both bituminous membrane and

metal flashings. At the eaves the membrane flashing is applied over 20-oz. lead-coated copper that extends 8 in. up the roof. This eaves flashing is bent so that it projects ⅜ in. over the uppermost piece of the cornice. This same flashing detail—membrane and metal—is also used at the gable ends where it runs along the rake from eaves to ridge.

The bituminous membrane extends down 1 ft. on both sides of the ridge. Over this is a metal cap flashing of 20-oz. lead-coated copper that runs 10 in. down both sides of the ridge. It was later covered with ridge shingles. A layer of Ice & Water Shield extends 3 ft. on both sides of the valleys. And then, as we shingled the valleys with the 18-in. red-cedar roof shingles, we step flashed each course with 18-in. diamond-shaped pieces of membrane flashing. The hips were done in a similar fashion, using smaller diamonds.

Following the architect's specifications for the flashing details was time-consuming and at some point seemed to be overkill. But after numerous brutal winter storms, the house remains tight to the weather.

After the house was completed, I drove out to the site during a hurricane. As I stood in the living room, nothing stirred, nothing creaked. The only noise was the wind rushing over the top of the chimney, sounding like a jet engine.

Teak, Mahogany and Stainless Steel

The different woods used on the exterior of the house were chosen for both their beauty and durability. Red-cedar shingles were used on the roof, and white cedar was picked for the sidewalls. The 11,582 lin. ft. of exterior trim, which includes rakes, cornices, belt course and water tables, is mahogany (see the photos on the facing page). Exterior handrails, newel posts and staircase, as well

Two miles of trim. More than 11,000 lin. ft. of wood, including teak, mahogany and redwood, was used for the running trim outside the house. The trim includes cornices that were radiused, curved and mitered. All of the trim was biscuited, glued with epoxy and fastened with square-drive stainless-steel screws.

Classical Details in a Harsh Environment **113**

as the 13,220 lin. ft. of exterior quartersawn decking are all teak.

All doors and windows were designed by the architect and fabricated for this project. The exterior doors—12 French doors, five panel doors and their accompanying screen doors—are constructed of pattern-grade mahogany. Pattern-grade wood is considered to be the most defect-free of all grades. The 35 tilt-turn windows and the five casement units are also built with pattern-grade mahogany. This grade of wood was used because the owners wanted the exteriors of all doors and windows to have a natural look with a clear finish. A lesser grade of wood would have imperfections that would mar the finish surface.

All of the running trim was installed with stainless-steel screws. Screws have superior holding power over nails, but there was another reason we used them for the trim. Using screws enabled us to dry-fit the myriad pieces of cornice, columns, water tables and scotia. Because we were working to the highest standards and the smallest tolerances, we had to be able to dismantle easily any of the hundreds of trim components and adjust a particular cope or miter until the joints were perfect. All of our end-to-end joints are scarfed and biscuited and glued with a two-part West System epoxy glue (see sources). When we were working in the cold, we added a hardener that accelerates the curing process of the glue. More than two years after the completion of the construction, all joints remain perfectly tight.

Numerous times during construction we were asked by the owners or the architect to build a full-scale mock-up of a trim detail on the house for inspection (see the photo at left). Although it was time-consuming work, both the architect and the client were thoroughly satisfied with the final results. There were no surprises.

No surprises with full-scale mock-ups. A porch cornice is mocked up with the full-scale profile of a tapered column (cut from 1x stock) set in place for final approval from the architect and the client. This ensured that there would be no surprises when the porches were flanked by 24 columns (see the photo on p. 117).

Porches and Decks

The floors of the decks and the covered porches are made of 1-in. by 2⅛-in. quartersawn teak with slightly eased edges. On the covered porches, the floors are mirrored by the porch ceilings. The ceiling stock is ¾-in. by 2¾-in. mahogany with chamfered edges. Unlike the porch and deck floors, which are left natural, the porch ceilings are painted.

Because of the long, continuous runs of ceiling stock, the eye might pick up slight deviations in the coursing. Therefore, the long runs are broken intermittently by 6-in. wide boards that run perpendicular to the ceiling.

To guarantee that our courses for the long runs of porch ceilings and porch and deck floors remained straight—the deck on

Curved cornice in an eyebrow dormer. The focal point of the house's ocean-side facade is the large, 40-lite kitchen window seen here from the interior (photo at left) and the exterior (photo below). The curved five-piece exterior cornice terminates in bracketed water tables.

the ocean side is 83 ft. long—we strung monofilament fishing line along the framing as a reference line. Monofilament can be strung very tightly, and it doesn't stretch or sag the way nylon masons string might. Monofilament's small diameter allowed us to work to high tolerances.

The porch ceilings contain two continuous vents that ventilate the roof system. The vents are screened with stainless steel, and all ceiling framing members were painted flat black so that they would not be visible.

Perhaps one of the most striking features of the house is the arched kitchen window (see the photos above). The construction of the rough opening and the assembly of the window unit as it came to us from the millwork shop presented quite a challenge. The unit itself is made of three rectangular, tilt-turn sash and three curved, fixed sash above. The five-piece cornice at the head of this massive window is curved; the two ends of the curve terminate in bracketed water tables.

Plywood header. The header for the arch top kitchen window is made of seven layers of ¾-in. plywood cut to fit the window's curves.

SOURCES

For Ice & Water Shield:
W. R. Grace Construction
800-444-6459
www.graceconstruction.com

For West System epoxy glue:
Gougeon Brothers, Inc.
517-684-7286
www.gougeon.com

If the window was installed in a flat wall, the installation would have been fairly straightforward. The rough opening complicated things because it incorporates a 3-in-12 pitch eyebrow dormer that ends flush with the sidewall. We built the header out of seven layers of ¾-in. plywood. Each piece was cut to the curve of the window arch as well as to the angle of the dormer pitch (see the photo above).

Another area of the exterior that tested everyone's layout and assembly skills was the installation of the 14 redwood Tuscan columns and their attendant teak handrails (see the photo on the facing page).

The columns were shipped in halves, which were joined on site around a pressure-treated 4x4 post. We used West System epoxy resin glue to join the column halves together, and 1,000-lb. test nylon band clamps were used to hold the column halves together as the glue cured.

The joint where the top handrail meets the column had to be coped to the radius of the column. The joint is demanding

enough where the column is straight, but these columns taper top to bottom. There was a good deal of filing to get a perfect fit.

The construction of this house has been the greatest learning experience of my many years working as a residential contractor. The expertise and assistance from the architect throughout the construction process made an enormously complex job proceed without difficulty. This was a project that depended upon the coordinated collaboration of dozens of players: the architectural staff, the project supervisor, the carpenters, the subcontractors, as well as all material suppliers. The building stands as a testament to this cooperative effort, and each time I visit I am impressed by the beauty and the integrity of what the joint effort produced.

Robert Weinstein is the principal of Roberts Associates Builders, Inc., in Truro, MA. In addition to *Fine Homebuilding*, his work has appeared in *Architectural Digest* and *Design Solutions, Journal of the Architectural Woodwork Institute.*

The different woods used on the exterior of the house were chosen for both their beauty and durability.

Visible along the outside edge of the porch ceiling are the unobtrusive vents for the roof system.

Restoring Flaggship

THE ISLAND OF NANTUCKET IS FAMOUS FOR ITS working-class whaling and fishing history, yet its windswept shores have drawn well-heeled summer vacationers for more than a century. One of the precursors to today's building boom dates back to 1883, when a Boston developer named William Flagg acquired a large tract of oceanfront property that he promptly subdivided into 85 building lots. Other members of the social elite quickly snapped up these lots and built simple cottages to which they could flee from the heat of the city. Although these cottages all were charming examples of late-Victorian architecture, Flaggship, the Second Empire-style house Flagg built for himself, stood out because of its mansard roof and decorative shingle work.

In recent years many of these fine structures have been torn down to make room for modern summer mansions. Flaggship was headed for a similar fate until its next-door neighbors decided to restore the cottage to use as a guesthouse. As architects who specialize in historic restoration, we were called in to make it happen.

Old Photos and a Similar Cottage Help to Re-Create the Past

Like most old houses, Flaggship had suffered its share of inappropriate alterations over the years. The task that our clients set for us was twofold: first, to bring back the charm of the original summer cottage; and second, to add in the modern conveniences that would allow the house to be occupied (comfortably) all year round.

Like many summer cottages of the time, Flaggship was built without a finished interior. Beadboard exterior sheathing and exposed framing members served as the interior finish. This type of construction—essentially a wooden tent—is comfortable for summer living but is largely uninhabitable

False framing conceals modern comforts while re-creating the character of this historic summer cottage. Photos of the original cottage inspired the restoration of Flaggship (inset). Rockers on the front porch still beckon guests to sit and relax.

Structural modifications enliven the main floor. With the removal of the central fireplace (located where the china cabinet is now), a rabbit warren of tiny rooms was transformed into an expansive party space. The traditional look of the beamed ceiling disguises the structural steel that supports the second floor. Photo taken at B on floor plan.

The task was twofold: bring back the charm of the original summer cottage; and add modern conveniences.

during the remainder of the year. Previous owners had winterized the structure by insulating the walls and covering the framing with drywall and simple trim. Although this modern solution had to go, all concerned knew that we could never go back to bare studs, at least not on the first floor.

Our clients had seen an interior in a neighboring structure, named Sunnycliff, that they thought would be appropriate. Approximately the same age as Flaggship, Sunnycliff was built with finished wood paneling on the walls and ceilings. With slight modifications, this original finish provided the model for the first-floor interior detail (see the photo above).

Re-creating the exterior of Flaggship became easier after we stumbled upon photographs, taken shortly after the house was built, at the Nantucket Historical Association

(see the photo on p. 118). Through these photographs, we learned that the symmetrical character of the original cottage had been altered early in the 20th century by the addition of an open porch to the south. Much later in the century, an enclosed library was added to the north side of the cottage. To restore the symmetry of the original house, our clients decided to remove the library addition and replace it with an open porch identical to the one on the south side (see the photo on p. 119).

Scalloped Shingles Match Originals

Besides the additions, the most obvious alteration to Flaggship's exterior was the loss of the original scalloped-pattern cedar-shingle roof. At some point, the lower roof had been replaced with square cedar shingles, and the upper roof had been replaced with green asphalt shingles. This combination resulted in an unpleasant two-tone appearance. After stripping the asphalt roofing and replacement shingles, we replicated the original roofing in ⅝-in. butt, fire-resistant red-cedar shingles. The scalloped-pattern shingles around the lower roof section and in the gables of the dormers were ripped to a common width and precut along a curved pattern on a bandsaw. We then applied the pattern shingles to the building to match the original photographs, using Cedar Breather from Benjamin Obdyke Inc. under the new roofing to provide ventilation and to increase the longevity of the shingles (see sources on p. 127).

As part of the old winterization scheme, the original single-glazed windows had been covered with mill-finished aluminum storms. To eliminate the need for storm windows, we had new windows and doors custom-fabricated by Dover Windows and Doors (see sources) to match the originals. All these units incorporate modern weather-stripping and double-insulated glass. To maintain the historic character of the glass, we specified Restoration Glass by Bendheim Glass Co. (see sources) for the inner pane of the double glazing (see the top photo at right).

Fireplace Had to Go, But the Chimney Remains

One of the biggest dilemmas we faced with the exterior renovation was what to do with the central chimney. As important as the chimney was to crown the peaked mansard roof, its central location in the plan subdivided the interior into a number of small spaces. To create a more open floor plan, we removed the existing winder stairway that cut the living room in half and placed a custom-built circular staircase between the

The look (but not the feel) of old glass. Although the windows and doors are double-glazed for energy efficiency, their inner panes are specially made to re-create the wavy look of historic glass. Photo taken at E on floor plan.

Elegant and efficient. A custom-built circular staircase provides access to bedrooms without taking up much space. A full-height baluster screen separates the stairway from the kitchen without impeding the flow of sunlight. Photo taken at C on floor plan.

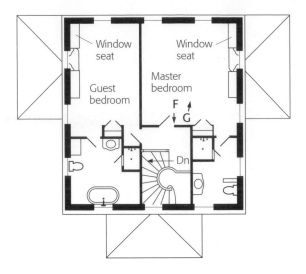

Room Enough for the Whole Family
A wide-open floor plan on the main floor coupled with a full-size finished basement provides plenty of space for entertaining or for putting up guests.

Window seat

Guest bedroom

Window seat

Master bedroom

F

G

Dn

Old library additions (remodeled)

Dining room

Living room

D

B

E

C

Kitchen

Up

Pantry

Sunroom entry

North

0 2 4   8 ft.

Photos taken at lettered positions.

SPECS

BEDROOMS: **3**

BATHROOMS: **3½**

SIZE: **2,634 sq. ft.**

COST: **N/A**

COMPLETED: **2000**

LOCATION: **Siasconset, Massachusetts**

ARCHITECT: **Bentley & Churchill Architects**

DESIGNER/BUILDER: **Michael Phillips Construction**

Laundry

Recreation room

Bedroom

Up

main entrance and the kitchen (see the bottom photo on p. 121). But that wasn't enough: The owners insisted that the fireplace had to go, though the chimney could remain. Our solution was to create a false chimney that, in addition to its aesthetic function, hides the remote exhaust fans that serve the two full baths on the second floor. To construct the chimney, we framed a weatherproof plywood box into the roof and covered it with cement backerboard. We then cut used bricks to ½-in. thickness and stuck them to the backerboard with thinset mortar.

Structural and Aesthetic Framing Re-Create Historical Character

Like many Victorian-era houses, Flaggship's original framing would be considered light by modern codes. The house was supported by a system of 4x6 wooden girders that rested atop shallow, native-stone piers. To stabilize the foundation and to prevent movement, we propped up the entire structure on a system of steel beams, elevated to allow the construction of a full-basement foundation beneath.

Steel beams, added to support the second floor, were trimmed in wood to panelize the first-floor ceiling (see the photo on p. 120). Inspired by the interiors in Sunnycliff, the panels between the beams were trimmed in a rail-and-stile frame with a recessed panel of beadboard. We employed a similar detail for the vertical beaded wall paneling at the baseboard and frieze to complete the historic interior finish.

The original roof framing was held together by 2x4 collar ties located at the break in the (double-pitched) mansard roof. Although structurally sound, this arrangement resulted in claustrophobically low ceilings in each of the second-floor bedrooms. To enhance the feeling of spacious-

Decorative Framing Conceals Insulation

After the mansard roof was insulated, a layer of beadboard sheathing
was applied over the framing. Then a false 2x4 frame was built onto the sheathing.
The result: bedrooms and baths that provide the emotional warmth of a rustic cottage,
but not the physical chill.

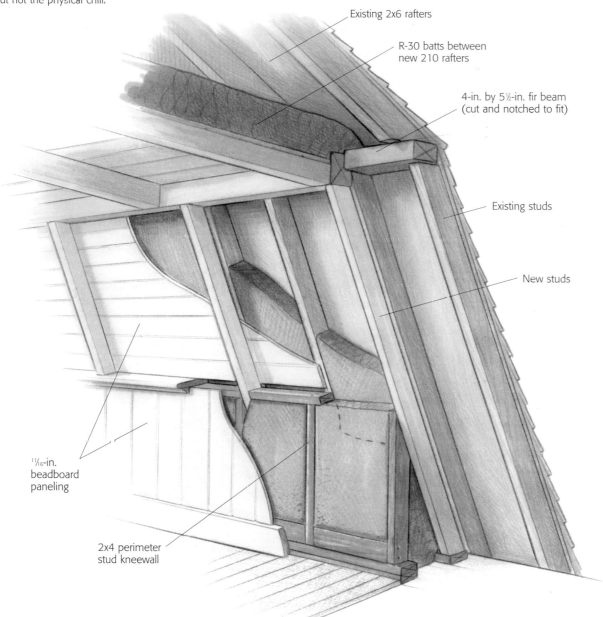

Existing 2x6 rafters

R-30 batts between
new 210 rafters

4-in. by 5½-in. fir beam
(cut and notched to fit)

Existing studs

New studs

$^{11}\!/_{16}$-in.
beadboard
paneling

2x4 perimeter
stud kneewall

ness and to restore a camp-like atmosphere, we took out the existing ceiling and installed a new vaulted ceiling over the entire second floor but didn't stop there. We applied a layer of beadboard paneling beneath the new ceiling framing and ran out a false work of 2x4 studs beneath the paneling (see the drawing above). The effect of this framing simulates the original appearance of exposed framing and sheathing. In addition to insulation and wiring,

the attic space above the ceiling conceals plumbing vents (which consolidate with the original stack) and remote bathroom fans that vent through the false chimney.

Modern Comforts are Well Hidden

Although insulation and state-of-the-art doors and windows help to keep the heat in, year-round comfort is assured through

Camp Granada, this isn't.
A false work of exposed sheathing and framing gives the fully insulated master bedroom the appearance of a rustic summer camp. Photo taken at G on floor plan.

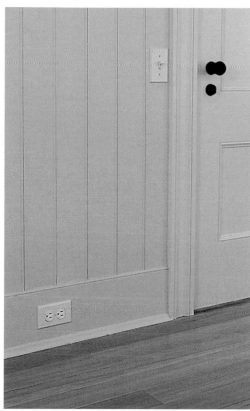

Hiding an eyesore. To make sure that modern electrical fixtures don't attract undue attention, the author mounts duplex receptacles in the baseboards and places wall switches in line with the doorknobs. Photo taken at F on floor plan.

the addition of a propane-fired, radiant under-floor heating system. Kick-space blowers housed under cabinetry in the kitchen and baths provide additional heat.

Old summer houses didn't have much in the way of cabinetry and built-ins, so throughout the house, these items are designed to appear as furniture. Bureaus and window seats in each of the upstairs bedrooms are built into the paneled wainscot (see the photo on the facing page). The bedroom closets are constructed to look like freestanding armoires.

Reproduction plumbing fixtures, including pedestal sinks and a claw-foot tub, furnish the upstairs bathrooms. Reconditioned period lighting fixtures and electrified antique kerosene lanterns discovered by the owners contribute to the appearance of antiquity. Electrical outlets are located horizontally in the baseboards—typical of houses built before electricity—with wall switches inconspicuously mounted low and

An open floor plan meant that the kitchen would become a focal point of the main living space and thus would have to be consistent with the historic character of the house.

adjacent to door hardware (see the top photo on p. 125).

Of course, the most difficult modern convenience to cover up was the kitchen. An open floor plan (see the floor plan on p. 122) meant that the kitchen would become a focal point of the main living space and thus would have to be consistent with the historic character of the house. Upper cabinets were eliminated in favor of open shelves on brackets (see the photo above). Built-in appliances, such as the dish-

washer, were shielded behind wood panels that match the cabinetry.

The owners' desire to eliminate the imposing mass of a full-height refrigerator was met by incorporating an undercounter Sub-Zero refrigerator and a pair of refrigerator drawers (see sources) beneath the central island (see the photo on the facing page). They chose a LaCornue range from Purcell Murray (see sources) that suggests the old kerosene ranges that once were standard in every summer cottage. Soapstone counter-

This house only looks old-fashioned. The kitchen includes period details throughout without compromising modern conveniences.

A camp kitchen with well-concealed modern conveniences. Despite the kitchen's rustic appearance, closer inspection reveals refrigeration units hidden beneath the island and a dishwasher tucked in beside the sink. Photo taken at D on floor plan.

SOURCES

Benjamin Obdyke Inc
800-346-7655
www.obdyke.com

Dover Windows and Doors
302-349-5070
www.doverwindows.com

Bendheim Glass Co.
800-221-7379
www.bendheim.com

Sub-Zero Freezer Co.
800-222-7820
www.subzero.com

Purcell Murray
800-892-4040
www.purcellmurray.com

tops with undermount sinks and routed drain boards also are similar to those commonly found in houses of the period.

Guests to Flaggship today find a turn-of-the-century summer cottage, frozen in time but with all the conveniences of home.

David Bentley and Elizabeth Churchill are partners in Bentley & Churchill Architects in Siasconset, MA. They have been designing and building custom homes on Nantucket Island since 1985. They have recently expanded their practice to include projects off island from their new winter office in Austin, TX.

One House at a Time

DAVE AND ROBIN KNIGHT ALWAYS THOUGHT IT WOULD BE a great experience to design and build a house for themselves and were jolted into action when their first daughter was born 27 years ago. After the house was done, they discovered that designing and building were so much fun that they embarked on a path that has continued to this day. Once they've lived in it for a little while, they put the family house up for sale, buy another lot, and start all over again. To date, they've built nine houses and two houseboats.

When we first met them 25 years ago, they were living in their 800-sq.-ft. cottage on remote Stuart Island, with two bouncy daughters, a huge wood-fired kitchen stove for heat and hand-built leaded-glass windows throughout. The house was small in scale and warm in spirit.

Over the years, their houses have matured. Each one is an evolutionary step from the prior project, polished and refined by direct, live-in-the-house experience. But even so, the country roots of that first house remain evident in all their projects.

1976—Steep, complicated roofs are a tradition. Built in 1976, the 1000-sq.-ft. Stuart Island house displays many of the elements of later projects, but less refined and at a smaller scale. All the houses have steep, complex roofs, with dormers and towers that make the upstairs bedrooms charming and quirky.

1998—Stone foundations look as if they've been there forever. The houses always have stony foundations that exert a visual gravity. In addition, each house is considered an opportunity to try out new materials. This home, the Smuggler's Cove house, was the first to include a thatch-style cedar-shingle roof.

2001—Separate spaces grafted together. Individual rooms take on their own identity by having their own roofs. Here, as in the prior houses, the dining room occupies its own hip-roofed alcove on a corner of the house. Photo taken at A on floor plan.

Blurred around the openings.
Instead of doorways, public rooms have generous openings where the contents of one spill into the next. In this dining room, for example, the kitchen counter wraps around the corner into the room. Photo taken at B on floor plan.

The "Patterns" of a Knight House

As a body of work, the Knights' houses reveal a collection of design ideas reused again and again, each in a slightly different way. Most of the photos presented here are from the Knights' latest project, the Garrison Bay house. Two other houses, the Smuggler's Cove house and the Stuart Island house, demonstrate how the patterns recur and take different shape (see the photos on pp.128–129).

Interior Spaces Influence the Exterior Look. Some of the spaces are conceived of as separate volumes with their own roofs, which then are welded into the bulk of the house. These special rooms often are located at the corners, such as a dining alcove on an exterior corner for a better view. This design also can work in reverse, such as using an interior corner for an entry alcove, which can provide better protection from the elements (see the floor plans on p. 134). This approach results in an unusually complex perimeter and roof.

The Major Rooms Overlap One Another. Instead of doorways from one space to another, the rooms have fuzzy edges where they commingle. For example, the dining room is part of the kitchen (see the photo at left), and the den is open to the living area. The result is longer views and a sense of inclusion.

The Roofs Are Complex and Steep. They come low to the ground in places, strongly sheltering the building and defining the profile of the house. The slopes of the various roofs are not necessarily equal. These roofs hold the second-floor rooms, giving a purpose to their steepness and producing interesting secondary dormers and towers.

The Scale Is Related to the Human Body. The houses have a balance to their scale. They're not too big and not too small. The feeling is intimate but uncrowded. Heavy timbers and stone give them a substantial bearing that is also snug and cozy, such as the living room at the Garrison Bay house (see the photos on the facing page).

The Rocks of the Building Flow into the Gardens. The surrounding landscape is integrated with the house and defined by retaining walls, pools and planting borders built of the same rock as the house (see the photo on p. 129).

Comfort in a weighty presence.
Cantilevered atop hefty beams, the balcony pulpit in the Garrison Bay house overhangs a portion of the living room. Photo taken at C on floor plan.

The stone fireplace cascades down the wall to merge with larger boulders arranged as a hearthside sitting area. Photo taken at D on floor plan.

... they want to make their houses look as though the houses came from another era, when talented artisans could spend the time necessary to make one-of-a-kind buildings.

Details at every level. Curved bargeboards and brackets frame the balcony off the master bedroom. Photo taken at E on floor plan.

The Houses Are Chunky and Massive. They hug the site tightly, growing out of the rocky landscape with massive rock bases and rock chimneys. The windowsills are deep. The overall effect is one of solidity, strength and security. Similarly, the houses incorporate heavy exposed timbers for posts and beams (see the photo above). The timbers are essential to making the houses feel as though they are a part of the Pacific Northwest woods.

The Houses Delight in Decorative Features. Each house is a chance for the Knights to demonstrate their respect for the materials and to invest the house with craftsmanship. And they do so at every scale, from leaded glass decoratively subdivided into small panes to shaped rafter ends, from intricate stucco patterns to roofs capped with ridge vents and tower finials (see the photo on the facing page).

Decorative features are the rule. The builders see each house as an opportunity to add layers of detail in appropriate places. On this slate roof, for example, copper ridge caps and pointy finials provide the finishing touches.

THE GARRISON BAY HOUSE

Although the sites change, some patterns are repeated in each Knight house. For one, the dining space
is always on an outside corner in a room that jogs out from the house so that it can have its own roof shape.
Another recurring pattern is the entry at an inside corner, where shelter is provided by the wing of the building.

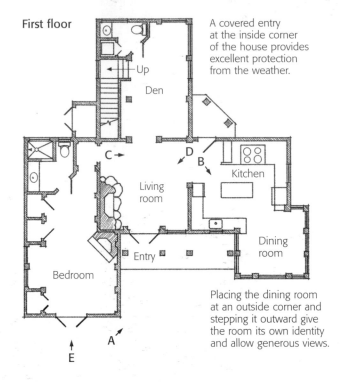

First floor

A covered entry
at the inside corner
of the house provides
excellent protection
from the weather.

Up

Den

C →

Living
room

D

B

Kitchen

Entry

Dining
room

Bedroom

A

E

Placing the dining room
at an outside corner and
stepping it outward give
the room its own identity
and allow generous views.

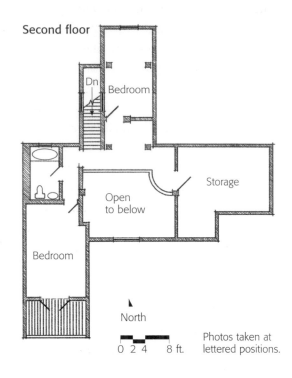

Second floor

Dn

Bedroom

Open
to below

Storage

Bedroom

North

0 2 4   8 ft.

Photos taken at
lettered positions.

---

*Once they've lived
in it for a little
while, they put the
family house up for
sale, buy another
lot, and start all
over again.*

Minimum Plans, Maximum Craft

When it's time to begin the next house, Dave and Robin start with floor-plan sketches tailored to the site but without regard for exterior appearance. The latest house, for example, is built on an unusually small, narrow lot, but one with a shallow-bank water access and a wonderful view across Garrison Bay.

The plan is straightforward, arranged to provide the view in most of the major rooms (see the floor plan above). The dining room and downstairs bedroom flank a patio on the view side, creating a partial courtyard. Along the backside, a den is extended into the hillside to help shape an entry court at the inside-corner intersection. Upstairs bedrooms are tucked under the roofs and reached by way of an upstairs balcony that overlooks the living room.

Once the plan is settled, the Knights build a balsa-wood model of the main structural framework at ½-in. scale. This model is their most powerful tool for working out the roof intersections and imagining what the shape of the building will look like from the outside.

They do no further drawings of elevations, sections or details. Instead, they hand over the sketch and model to a local architect for drafting and structural engineering. The goal is to secure the most basic no-frills documents for a construction permit: no interior elevations, no appliances or bath fixtures, no material textures on the exterior elevations, no details.

The Knights claim (with a little tongue in cheek) that once construction begins, the drawings are put away in a drawer and never consulted again. They explain that one of the real joys of their style of work is that detail decisions can be instinctive and that changes can be made on site, in response to the reality of the developing house. As architects, we are both delighted and horrified to hear this, applauding the Knights' flexibility and sensitivity to the need for responsiveness, crestfallen to hear how casually they regard the work of our profession.

Once the house is under way, they do all the work themselves. Well, almost all of it. They subcontract insulation and drywall. Otherwise, they enjoy the act of building, and they want to make their houses look as though the houses came from another era, when talented artisans could spend the time necessary to make one-of-a-kind buildings. (see the photos at right). One reason they can pull this off is that ten years ago, the Knights were joined by Dave Brand, the son they never had. Little Dave has become an integral part of the team, making possible larger, more ambitious houses.

Spontaneity and New Materials

Changes during construction are almost guaranteed when the working drawings are minimal. And in a way, that's part of the attraction of being both designers and builders, because changes can make the building better.

For example, the upstairs balcony appeared on the plans to allow direct access to the storage room. But once the rafters were in place, it became apparent that inadequate headroom made entry awkward. The solution was a curved bump-out that not only eased entry to the storage room but also created an attractive "pulpit" overlooking the living room (see the photo at right on p. 131).

Each house incorporates a new element, never tried before, and sometimes this new element pops up once the house is under construction. In this case, the Knights

The hand-troweled stucco below the balcony supports has the look of heavy impasto.

The homeowners never miss an opportunity to use natural, decorative elements. At special corners, fitted boulders support posts.

decided to install a slate roof (see the photo on p. 133). It was heavy enough to require re-engineering and modification of the roof structure during construction. And the steepness and complexity of the roof made for a lengthy installation: four months. But the Knights claim they will do it again on their next house. Either that, or maybe a thatched roof—the only roof that might actually take longer than a slate roof to install.

Max Jacobson and Helen Degenhardt are partners in the Berkeley architectural firm JSW/D Architects. Jacobson is a co-author of *A Pattern Language*, *The Good House*, and most recently, *Patterns of Home*, published by The Taunton Press, Inc. (2002).

Credits

The articles compiled in this book appeared in the following issues of *Fine Homebuilding*:

p. ii: Photo © Bill Sanders.

p. v: Photo by Charles Miller, courtesy *Fine Homebuilding,* © The Taunton Press, Inc.

Table of Contents: p. vi (top to bottom)—photos by Roe A. Osborn, Charles Bickford, Charles Miller, Scott Gibson, courtesy *Fine Homebuilding,* © The Taunton Press, Inc.; p. vii (top to bottom) photos by Tom O'Brien, John Phelps, Warren Jagger, Jefferson Kolle, courtesy *Fine Homebuilding,* © The Taunton Press, Inc.

p. 2: Photo by Roe A. Osborn, courtesy of *Fine Homebuilding,* © The Taunton Press, Inc.

p. 4: Seattle Eclectic by Lane Williams, issue 109. Photos on pp. 4 & 7 by Fred Housel; Photos on pp. 5, 9, 10 & 11 by Laurie Black; Illustration on p.6 by Mark Hannon; Illustration on p.8 by Lane Williams.

p. 12: Dueling Towers on the Carolina Coast by Chuck Dietsche, issue 109. Photos by Roe A. Osborn, courtesy of *Fine Homebuilding,* © The Taunton Press, Inc.; Illustration by Mark Hannon.

p. 20: Building by the Water by Jeremiah Eck, issue 114. Photos on pp. 20, 23, 24 & 26 by Charles Bickford, courtesy of *Fine Homebuilding,* © The Taunton Press, Inc.; Photos on pp. 21 & 27 by Anton Grassl (www.atongrassl.com); Illustration by Vince Babak.

p. 28: Little House with Rich Spaces by Barry Griblin, issue 86. Photos by Charles Miller, courtesy of *Fine Homebuilding,* © The Taunton Press, Inc., except p. 32 Photo © Barry Griblin; Illustrations by Christopher Clapp.

p. 34: The House on the Windy Beach by Charles Miller, issue 147. Photos by Charles Miller, courtesy of *Fine Homebuilding,* © The Taunton Press, Inc.; Illustrations by Mark Hannon.

p. 44: Block Island Boat House by Bryan K. Wilson, issue 122. Photos by Roe A. Osborn, courtesy of *Fine Homebuilding,* © The Taunton Press, Inc., except p. 46 Photo by Robert M. Downie; Illustration by Mark Hannon.

p. 50: A House Shaped by Its Site by Michael McNamara, issue 107. Photos by Kevin Ireton, courtesy of *Fine Homebuilding,* © The Taunton Press, Inc.; Illustrations by Vince Babak except p. 57 (top) Illustration by Michael McNamara.

p. 60: Mango House by Peter Mullen, issue 85. Photos by Scott Gibson, courtesy of *Fine Homebuilding,* © The Taunton Press, Inc., except p. 66 Photo by Peter Mullen; Illustrations by Jeff Bellantuono.

p. 68: Guest House by the Bay by Peter Zimmerman, issue 131. Photos by Tom O'Brien, courtesy *Fine Homebuilding,* © The Taunton Press, Inc.; Illustrations by Scott Bricher.

p. 76: A Coastal Remodel Triumphs Over Limits by Duo Dickinson, issue 144. Photos by Chris Green, courtesy *Fine Homebuilding,* © The Taunton Press, Inc.; Illustrations by Ron Carboni.

p. 84: Detailing Decks Over Living Space by John Phelps, issue 112. Photo by John Phelps; Illustration by Christopher Clapp.

p. 88: The Bridge House by James Estes, issue 101. Photos on pp. 88, 91(top) & 95 by Warren Jagger; Photos on pp. 91 (bottom), 92-94 by Charles Miller, courtesy *Fine Homebuilding,* © The Taunton Press, Inc.; Illustrations by Mark Hannon.